FURNITURE FUNDAMENTALS

Tables

POPULAR WOODWORKING BOOKS

CINCINNATI, OHIO

popularwoodworking.com

Contents

Traditional Drop-Leaf Table

BY JOHN TATE

To cut the tenons, use a dado stack on the table saw. Reduce the tenon in thickness by $3/16$" on each side.

Cut $1/2$" shoulders on each side of the aprons.

You will need to fasten the tabletop using tabletop fasteners, which requires making a kerf in the aprons. I made this kerf on the table saw $7/16$" from the edge and $1/4$" deep.

I n our living room, we keep a mahogany table that I vaguely knew one of my ancestors had built. After I began my internship at *Popular Woodworking*, I became more interested in that table. I asked my paternal grandmother about the table, and she told me that my great-great-grandfather, Carl Edward Wulff, built it at his furniture shop in downtown Cincinnati about 1870. She even had a photograph of his shop dated 1878. In the picture you can see the simple sign that says "Furniture."

With this proof, I knew that woodworking was definitely in my blood. Having the family tradition in mind, I set about building a slightly simplified facsimile. In fact, the joinery in this project is so simple that almost any beginner can do it.

Start With the Basics

After cutting all your rough stock to length, surface your wood down to $3/4$" thick (except for the legs). The original 19th-century table's top was only one board. You can still find mahogany in these widths, but I couldn't. To obtain the appropriate width, I had to glue up two boards for both the leaves and the tabletop. I used three biscuits at each joint to keep the boards aligned during glue-up. Also, if you can't get $2 1/4$"-thick stock for the legs, ask for turning blanks at the lumber store instead; you might just get lucky.

Mortises, Tenons & Tapers

The first step is to make mortise-and-tenon joints where the aprons join the legs. I made the tenons using a dado stack on the table saw. Cut the shoulders as shown in the photo above. Make the tenons $3/8$" thick, 1" long and $3 1/4$" wide. After cutting your tenons, cut a groove in the aprons for the tabletop fasteners, which will attach the top to the table's base. Make this slot by cutting a kerf in the aprons that's $7/16$" down from the top edge. For a nice detail, I routed a bead on the bottom edge of the aprons.

The mortises on all the legs are made $1 7/16$" from the inside for the short aprons and $7/16$" from the inside for the long aprons as shown in the diagram on the next page. Cut your mortises on the legs; I used a mortiser, but you can use a chisel or Forstner bit.

The original table had turned legs, but in order to simplify things, I tapered the legs. Tapering jigs for the table saw can be tricky, so I used a band saw to cut the tapers about $1/16$" shy of my line and then cleaned up the cut on the jointer. The taper should start 1" below where

the aprons end and result in a leg that tapers to one-half the original thickness. Remember: Taper only the sides that have mortises.

Install the Hinges

After tapering, sand the legs and aprons. Start with #100-grit sandpaper, move up to #150-grit, then finish with #220-grit. Next, glue up the legs and aprons and clamp.

After gluing up the base, turn your attention to the top. Install the hinges that connect the tabletop to the leaves. Use two on each side, and place them $7 1/4$" inches from the end to allow room for the leaf supports.

Lay out the location of the hinges by first placing a $1/16$" spacer (I used pieces of plastic laminate) between the leaf and tabletop.

Clamp the pieces together, put the hinges down and trace them with a pen-

I made the mortises using a mortiser. In order to form the holes more safely, you should think of the path of least resistance. Instead of just going in a straight line from left to right or right to left, make two holes with a slight gap between. Then clear out the gap. If you simply work in a straight line, the mortiser's chisel could bend or break.

cil. Use a router with a straight bit to hog out most of the area. Then use a chisel to define the corners. Install the hinges and make sure they work properly.

A 4" radius on the outside corners of the leaves on the original table was a nice touch. In order to re-create this, I traced the curve from the original and made a template using a piece of plywood.

Cut the shape to size on a band saw and then use the template with a router and straight bit to finish the radius.

Make the Leaf Supports
To keep the leaves upright, assemble two supports for each side. These are basically two pieces of wood finger-jointed together to form a "knuckle" joint hinge.

The ½" knuckle joints are made on a table saw using a finger-jointing jig. Round the edges of the "fingers" with a rasp or sandpaper so the joint pivots. Then drill a ¼" hole through the fingers and tap a ¼" dowel in place. Instant wooden hinges. One note: You'll have to cut a notch in the two supports so they'll clear the hinge barrels on the top. Mark the location of the notch when you dry-assemble the table. The angle cuts on the supports form a triangular hole against the apron. Cut a triangular piece of mahogany to fill this space, being careful not to let the filler rub against the supports. For simplicity, you may use brass hinges instead of knuckle joints.

Sanding and Finishing
Remove the hinges from the tabletop and sand the table. Because the top will be the most visible surface, I chose to go up to #220 grit. The bottom requires only #150 grit. In order to simplify finishing,

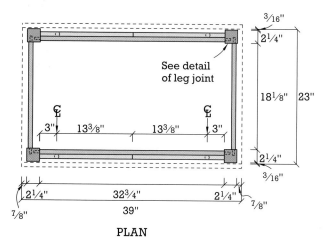

PLAN

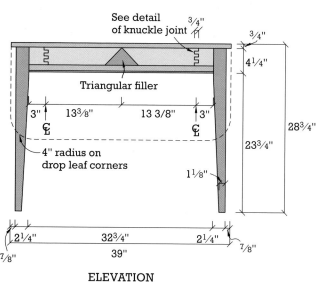

ELEVATION

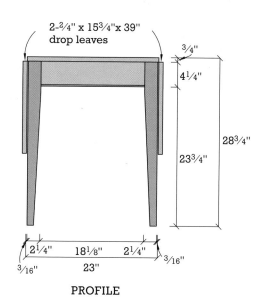

PROFILE

Traditional Drop-Leaf Table

NO.	ITEM	DIMENSIONS (INCHES)			MATERIAL	COMMENTS
		T	W	L		
1	Tabletop	³/₄	23	39	Mahogany	
2	Leaves	³/₄	15³/₄	39	Mahogany	
4	Legs	2¼	2¼	28	Mahogany	
2	Short aprons	³/₄	4¼	20⅛	Mahogany	1" TBE; ¼" offset
2	Long aprons	³/₄	4¼	34³/₄	Mahogany	1" TBE; 1¼" offset
4	Leaf supports	³/₄	3¼	18*	Mahogany	
2	Triangles	³/₄	3¼	6½	Mahogany	

TBE = Tenon, both ends; *cut to fit

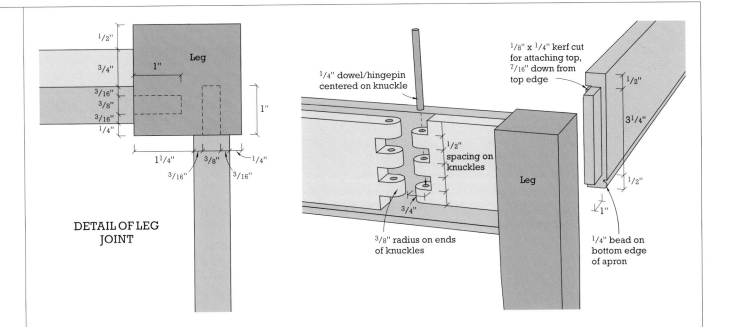

DETAIL OF LEG
JOINT

Leg

1"

1/2"

3/4"

3/16"
3/8"
3/16"
1/4"

1"

1 1/4"   3/8"   1/4"

3/16"   3/16"

1/4" dowel/hingepin
centered on knuckle

1/8" x 1/4" kerf cut
for attaching top,
7/16" down from
top edge

1/2"

1/2"
spacing on
knuckles

Leg

3/4"

3 1/4"

1/2"

1"

3/8" radius on ends
of knuckles

1/4" bead on
bottom edge
of apron

I waited to attach the supports until after finishing. This requires masking off the area where the support will be glued.

For the finish, I applied ZAR's 118 Dark Mahogany stain made by United Gilsonite Laboratories (visit www.ugl.com to find a retailer in your area). After letting the stain cure, I applied four coats of clear lacquer.

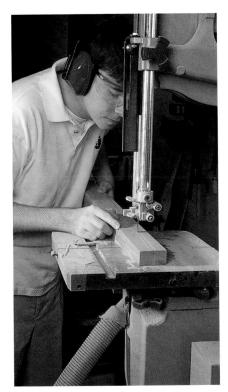

I tapered the legs on a band saw, then ran the legs over the jointer in order to make them smooth.

Final Construction Details

After the lacquer has dried, attach the supports and the triangle with glue and nails through the inside of the aprons. Place the top on the base and make sure the supports keep the leaves level. Now attach the top.

Because of the expansion and contraction of wood, you will need to attach the aprons to the tabletop using tabletop fasteners. The tabletop fasteners are installed by simply screwing the fasteners into place. Because the wood will move more in width than in length over time, be sure to leave more space on the long apron sides for the fasteners.

Overall, I was extremely pleased with the results of my project. I think my great-great-grandfather would be proud to know that I've continued the family tradition.

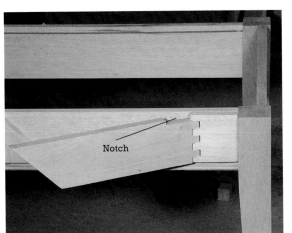

Notch

Supplies

Rockler
rockler.com or 800-279-4441

4 • Hinges for drop-leaves,
    item #29249, $11.99/pair

6 • Tabletop fasteners,
    item #34215, $2.99 for pack of 8

Prices as of publication date.

I made the leaf supports using a knuckle joint. You can see the notch I cut out in order to allow the leaf support to swing out past the hinge. Though optional, I thought the triangle rest in the center was a nice touch.

Country Settle Table

BY TROY SEXTON

When furniture was more precious to its owners, it was common for a piece to have more than one purpose in the household.

The settle table is a form that dates back to at least the Middle Ages, though some trace it back to a Roman form where even the base of the table folded flat. While it remained popular in early modern Europe, the settle table was quite common in colonial American homes. It combines the functions of table, chest and chair. In a home, it could be used as a table to serve the morning meal and then be converted to a chair and placed next to the hearth. In addition to creating a place to rest, the expansive back/top of the settle table also provided some shielding from the drafts of early American homes.

This version is typical in form and proportion to originals and is surprisingly straightforward to build. And like many of the originals, the base is painted but the top is not. Some furniture historians have speculated that the tops of these tables were also painted originally but were scrubbed clean so many times that they ended up as bare wood.

Slab and Dado Construction

The base is a simple box made from glued-up slabs of ¾"-thick poplar. The bottom rests in dados in the sides, and grooves in the front and back. The front and back are secured to the side pieces using an unusual joint that is both rabbeted and dovetailed. It's nothing difficult; even beginning woodworkers should find the joint easy to execute.

The top is also simple. The boards are joined using a tongue-and-groove joint. The rails on the underside are attached to the top using sliding dovetails.

Once you joint and plane all your material, glue up all the panels you need for the project and then begin construction by building the base.

One Big Dovetail

After cutting the pieces for the base to their finished width and length, begin by plowing a ¾"-wide × ¼"-deep shelf dado (as used in casework) in the side pieces that's 9½" up from the bottom edge of the sides. I use a dado stack in my table saw and guide the work against the fence. A router with a straight bit is another sound option.

You also need to cut a matching groove on the front and back pieces to hold the bottom. Cut the groove on the inside face of your front and back pieces beginning ½" up from the bottom edge of each piece.

Now comes a tricky part. You need to notch out the front and back edge of your side pieces to receive the front and back pieces. This ½"-deep notch begins at the dado you just cut for the bottom and runs 8¾" up the edge. You can cut this in a variety of ways, such as with a band saw or jigsaw. I do a lot of operations with my dado stack, so I secure the work to a miter gauge and run it on edge over the dado stack.

Set the side pieces aside and work on the front and back. To make the large

Here I'm beginning to cut the notches on the edges of the sides. With the work firmly against my miter gauge and an accessory fence, it's quite secure. If you have any trepidation about this technique, use a band saw or jigsaw.

I'm just about to begin cutting the dovetail portion on the notch. Here you can see the rabbet on the front and back pieces, plus the mating notches and the dados on the sides.

The rabbets on the front and back pieces also help you mark the joint on its mate. Press the tail board against your side pieces and mark the shape on the side. Then mark your cut lines on the inside and outside face of your side pieces.

The jigsaw is a two-handed tool. For maximum control, keep one hand on the tool and the other on the shoe when cutting the curves on the sides.

This is where you should take extra care when cutting. Cut it as close as you can and clean up the joint with a chisel if needed.

single dovetail on these pieces, the first step is to cut a ³⁄₄"-wide × ¹⁄₄"-deep rabbet on the ends. The shoulder of this rabbet adds strength and helps square the case during assembly.

The easiest way to cut the dovetail portion of this joint is with a few sure handsaw cuts. This is easy stuff, I assure you. First set your sliding T-bevel to 14° and mark out the shape of the male portion of the joint – the tail – on the front and back pieces.

Cut this with a backsaw – I use a Japanese dozuki – and clean up the cut and shoulder of the joint using a chisel.

Now transfer the shape of the dovetail onto the mating joint on your side pieces.

Use your backsaw to cut the female pin shape on your side pieces. Try to split the pencil line with your saw. Fit the pieces together and tweak the joint with a chisel until it goes together smoothly and firmly.

Dry fit all your joints and make sure the pieces can be assembled easily. Then

cut the curves on the side pieces. The cutout on the bottom is a 5" radius. The top corners of the sides are rounded at a 2¹⁄₄" radius. Cut these shapes with your jigsaw and smooth the cuts with coarse-grit sandpaper.

You don't need to cut the holes in the sides that will secure the top to the base yet; you'll bore those after the top is assembled.

Sand all your base parts and then glue up the base. Allow the bottom to float in its groove without glue. If you're going to paint your base, you can secure the joints with 18-gauge nails or cut nails for an authentic look.

The lid of the base is in two parts: the lid itself and a hinge board that is glued and nailed to the back of the base. Cut the hinge board to size so it fits tightly against the side pieces. Glue and nail it in place. To help support the lid, I recommend you glue and nail two lid supports to the sides so the lid will be supported at the sides as well as the front. Fit the lid to

the base and attach it to the hinge board with non-mortise hinges.

A Tippy Top

I made my top from four ⁷⁄₈"-thick boards that are cut to 50" long. Depending on what lumber you have available, you may need to use more boards. The top boards are joined using a close-fitting tongue-and-groove joint but no glue. The rails attached to the underside hold the top together with the help of some nails.

Begin by cutting a ¹⁄₄"-wide × ³⁄₈"-deep groove centered on one edge of each top board. Then cut a matching tongue on the mating edges. You want the fit to be close without splitting the joint.

Clamp up the top then lay out the location of the sliding dovetails that will secure the rails. Because this is a substantial cut, you should first rough out the dovetail socket with a straight bit – I made a ³⁄₈"-wide × ¹⁄₄"-deep dado that was 11¹⁄₂" from the end of each individual 50"-long board.

Country Settle Table

NO.	LET.	ITEM	DIMENSIONS (INCHES)			MATERIAL	COMMENTS
			T	W	L		
1	A	Top	⁷⁄₈	50	50	Poplar	Finishes at 48"
2	B	Top rails	⁷⁄₈	4³⁄₄	40⁵⁄₈	Poplar	¹⁄₄"-d. sliding dovetail
2	C	Sides	³⁄₄	17⁷⁄₈	28¹⁄₄	Poplar	
2	D	Front/back	³⁄₄	9¹⁄₂	25¹⁄₂	Poplar	Rabbet, both ends
1	E	Bottom	³⁄₄	16⁷⁄₈	24¹⁄₂	Poplar	Floats in groove
1	F	Lid	³⁄₄	15¹⁄₂	23⁷⁄₈	Poplar	
1	G	Lid hinge board	³⁄₄	2³⁄₄	24	Poplar	Nailed to back
2	H	Lid supports	³⁄₄	1¹⁄₂	15	Poplar	Nailed to sides

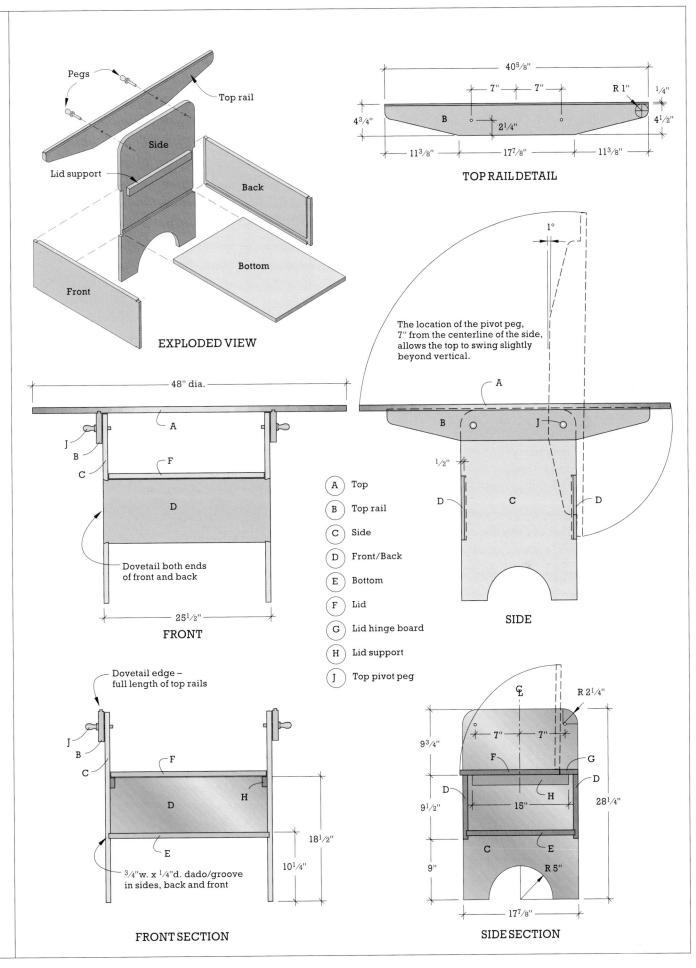

Pegs

Top rail

Side

Lid support

Back

Front

Bottom

EXPLODED VIEW

40⅝"

7" 7"

R 1"

¼"

B

2¼"

4¾"

4½"

11⅜" 17⅞" 11⅜"

TOP RAIL DETAIL

1°

The location of the pivot peg, 7" from the centerline of the side, allows the top to swing slightly beyond vertical.

48" dia.

A

J

B

C

F

D

Dovetail both ends of front and back

25½"

FRONT

A

B

J

½"

D

C

D

SIDE

A	Top	
B	Top rail	
C	Side	
D	Front/Back	
E	Bottom	
F	Lid	
G	Lid hinge board	
H	Lid support	
J	Top pivot peg	

Dovetail edge – full length of top rails

J

B

C

F

D

H

E

18½"

10¼"

¾"w. x ¼"d. dado/groove in sides, back and front

FRONT SECTION

CL

R 2¼"

9¾"

7" 7"

F

G

D

D

H

15"

9½"

C

E

9"

R 5"

28¼"

17⅞"

SIDE SECTION

Once you've cut the dados in the top pieces, install a ¾" dovetail bit with a 14° slope and repeat your cuts to make the angled shoulder on the top pieces.

Now re-assemble the top pieces and line up all the dovetail sockets. Cut your rails to size, then cut the mating dovetail joint on one long edge of the rails using the following steps.

Install the same dovetail bit in your router table and make test cuts on scrap until the fit between the male and female part of the joint is firm. Then machine the dovetail on one edge of each rail.

Now drill the holes for the pegs that will secure the rails to the base and allow the top to pivot. Their location and size is critical. First strike centerlines on the base and rails so you can line up the top and base easily before you drill the holes. The holes should be $^{25}/_{64}$" in diameter and their centers should be 7" from the centerline of the rails – this location allows the top to tip back just a little past 90° so it will stay upright. Then cut the rails to finished shape on your band saw; the ends have a 1" radius that tapers up to the full width of the rail.

Sand all your top components then assemble the rails and top without glue. Use Popsicle sticks to space the boards, then nail the rails in place through the top. Cut your top to finished size and shape using a jigsaw and then clean up your cuts with sandpaper.

Clamp the top on the base and use the holes in the rails as a guide to locate and drill the mating $^{25}/_{64}$" holes in the base. Add the four Shaker-style pegs from Horton Brasses (see the "Supplies" box) and construction is complete.

To finish this piece, I used a custom green color for the base that was picked out by the client who requested I build this piece. The top is painted on the underside and has a warm brown stain on the top. The entire project is then coated with lacquer.

What was most surprising about the entire project was sitting down in the completed piece. The entire time I was building this piece I was thinking, "This is probably not going to be a very comfortable chair."

On that point, I was wrong. It is a surprisingly nice place to sit and rest your bones, especially after a long day in the shop.

To cut dados and sliding dovetails, I like to use a shop-made template as shown here. With a template guide installed on my router, I can use the same template and template guide to make both the rough cut with a straight bit and the finish cut with a dovetail bit.

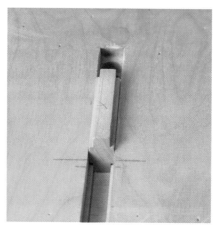

Because this is a common cut in my shop, I've also made a small block that allows me to confirm that the template, bit and template guide are all properly positioned to make the cut I'm after.

Make the dado cut on each board individually. If your parts are all the same length they'll line up just fine at assembly.

Assemble the top without glue on your bench, line up all the dovetail sockets and prepare your rail stock.

Fine-tune the fit of your rails by moving the fence a little in or a little out. And be sure to use the same dovetail bit for cutting this part of the joint that you used for the socket in the top.

Supplies

Horton Brasses
horton-brasses.com or 800-754-9127

4 • maple cupboard turn (pegs),
   item #WCT-4, $5.75 ea.

Lee Valley Tools
leevalley.com or 800-871-8158

2 • black, ball-tip, partial-wrap
   hinges, item #01H31.62, $4.30 ea.

Prices as of publication date.

Once you get the rails to fit in one dovetail socket, tweak the rail to fit across the entire top.

Draw-Leaf Game Table

BY GLEN D. HUEY

I was asked to design and build a gaming table. For me that is a table for playing pinochle or euchre, or a comfortable table for working a jigsaw puzzle with family members. So I set about working to accomplish my task by designing toward card-table dimensions when I stumbled across a television show of the "Texas hold 'em" card game. As I looked at the players spaced around the table I questioned the direction I had chosen.

I needed a design that could expand into a larger table. I needed leaves! But table leaves are a constant nuisance. If you need to store them away from the table, they take up too much closet space and are always getting dents and dings. If the leaves store in the table, you need to open it completely to install them.

Then I remembered a seldom-used design that could provide me with exactly what I was searching to find: the draw-leaf or Dutch pull-out table. In this design, the leaves store directly under the main top of the table and extend outward from each end when pulled from the table's base. The main top floats upward as the leaves are extended and will fit flush with the leaf when it is fully brought out. The fascinating aspect of this design is that the leaves may be extended even if the table is being used for the family puzzle. No need to remove anything from the top – just slide the leaves out!

Grab Your Scratch Pad

I began knowing I wanted the table to be 38" wide × 38¾" long and I wanted, for design purposes, a small amount of overhang – 1¼". This works because the smaller the overhang of the table, the wider the leaves will be. Next, I wanted to use a standard 24" for the distance from the floor to the bottom edge of the apron. This allows enough room to get one's legs comfortably under the table. Finally, knowing that the strength of a table is in the aprons, I wanted to use a 5½" apron to provide additional support. This would mean that my table would be 31" high while using two ¾"-thick tops – one for the leaves and one for the main top.

Given these measurements, I determined the sizes of my table's main components. Two ¾"-thick aprons along with the 1¼" overhang on both ends yields a total of 4". If you subtract that from the length of the top when closed, you have 34¾" remaining, which is the measurement of the inside of the base. From that you need to subtract the thickness of the stops (1") and the thickness of the center support (¾") and you have 32", which is the total that the table will extend. Divide that number by two to get the width of each individual leaf (16"). Finally, subtract the 32" from the closed length of 38¾" to get the fixed-top size of 6¾". With the numbers figured, we're ready to build.

A Base From Which to Build

The base is the place to begin with the construction of our table and I always begin with the legs. Not wanting to sim-

Cut the four flutes at the router table. The screw in the end of the leg blank helps to raise the blank from the bit to end the cut or to plunge into the correct position to begin the cut.

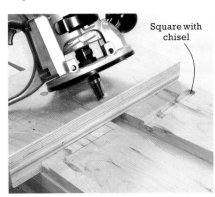

Use a square platform jig made from a few pieces of plywood and a pattern bit to cut the ¼"-deep dado for the center support.

Because one cheek of the apron's tenon is bare-faced, make a shoulder cut only on the apron's tenon face side of the piece.

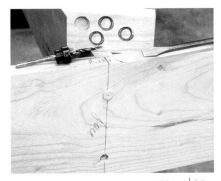

Use a tapered countersink and #8 × 1¼" screws to attach the center support, then fill the holes with matching face-grained plugs.

ply taper these legs, I opted to add flutes to the face sides. First, mill the leg blanks to size and mark the locations of the $\frac{3}{8}$"-wide × $4\frac{1}{2}$"-long × $1\frac{1}{4}$"-deep mortises. We are using a bare-face tenon joint, which means there is a shoulder only on one face of the apron. These mortises are located $\frac{3}{8}$" in from the face of each leg.

With the mortises complete, install a $\frac{1}{4}$" fluting bit into the router and set it so the bit makes only a cut $\frac{3}{16}$" wide. Place a line on your fence that is exactly centered with the middle of the fluting bit. I like to use the center of the bit to begin and end each cut rather than setting a line on each side of the bit to use as a starting or ending point.

Now draw a line at $\frac{7}{8}$" below the spot where the apron meets the leg. This line will be used to determine the top edge of the fluting. Next, you will need to lay out the locations of the flutes so they are evenly spaced across the face of each leg. Line up the bit with either of the middle flutes and set your fence.

Make two passes on each outside face of your legs. The first starts at the layout line and continues through the bottom edge of the leg. A second pass is made by reversing the leg and starting at the bottom edge, then stopping as the layout line matches with the line on your fence. This will create the two flutes on the inside of each leg. Next you need to reposition the fence to align the bit with either of the outside flute locations and repeat the steps. Afterward, the faces of each leg should have four flutes evenly spaced as shown in the photo on the previous page.

Work on the aprons begins by creating the tenons on the ends. Set the blade height to $\frac{3}{8}$" and position the fence to cut a $1\frac{1}{4}$"-long tenon. Because we're using bare-faced tenons you need to make the cut only on the face of the apron. Cut both ends of all four of the apron pieces. Then, without moving the fence, raise the depth of cut to $\frac{1}{2}$". Roll the aprons onto their edges and make the two cuts at each tenon to define the edge shoulders of the tenon.

Remove the remainder of the waste material on the tenons using the table saw, leaving the $\frac{3}{8}$"-thick tenon. At the band saw, set a straightedge fence in position to remove the $\frac{1}{2}$" of material on each side of the tenon. Because these tenons

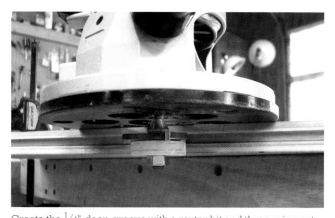

Create the $\frac{1}{4}$"-deep groove with a router bit and three-wing cutter. Run the cut from both faces of the plywood to ensure that it is centered.

Cut one end of your long edging stock at 45° and use the falloff, cut to the same angle, to find the exact position.

Draw-Leaf Game Table

NO.	ITEM	DIMENSIONS (INCHES)			MATERIAL	COMMENTS
		T	W	L		
4	Legs	$1\frac{3}{4}$	$1\frac{3}{4}$	$29\frac{1}{2}$	Cherry	
2	Long aprons	$\frac{3}{4}$	$5\frac{1}{2}$	$35\frac{1}{4}$	Cherry	$1\frac{1}{4}$" tenon, both ends
2	Short aprons	$\frac{3}{4}$	$5\frac{1}{2}$	$34\frac{1}{2}$	Cherry	$1\frac{1}{4}$" tenon, both ends
1	Center support	$\frac{3}{4}$	5	$34\frac{1}{2}$	Cherry	
1	Main top	$\frac{11}{16}$	36	$36\frac{3}{4}$	Plywood	Nominal $\frac{3}{4}$" plywood
2	Leaves	$\frac{11}{16}$	36	14	Plywood	Nominal $\frac{3}{4}$" plywood
1	Fixed top	$\frac{11}{16}$	36	$4\frac{3}{4}$	Plywood	Nominal $\frac{3}{4}$" plywood
5	Long edging	$\frac{11}{16}$	3	40	Cherry	Ea. makes 2 pcs.
3	Short edging	$\frac{11}{16}$	3	20	Cherry	Ea. makes 2 pcs.
4	Slides	$\frac{7}{8}$	$1\frac{1}{2}$	$36\frac{3}{4}$	Cherry	Cut to fit for length
1	Pierced brackets	$\frac{9}{16}$	$3\frac{1}{4}$	20	Cherry	Makes 8 pcs.
2	Apron moulding	$\frac{7}{8}$	2	40	Cherry	Ea. makes 2 pcs.
4	Stop blocks	$\frac{3}{4}$	$\frac{3}{4}$	$1\frac{1}{2}$	Poplar	
1	Locating dowel	$\frac{3}{4}$			Poplar	For top
1	Pinning dowel	$\frac{1}{8}$			Poplar	For brackets

Place the clamps on the bottom face of the plywood pieces to help protect the panel from damage or staining.

To sand the pieces flush, add pencil lines to the joint of the plywood and edging and when the lines disappear – the surface is level.

will touch in the center of the leg if left as-is, we need to cut a 45° angle onto each tenon. Make a single pass to cut the back edge of the tenon. Leave the length as long as possible.

The center base's support fits between the long aprons. To install the center support you need to create a $\frac{1}{4}$"-deep stopped dado located directly at the center of both aprons, into which the center support will slide. The dado is cut leaving $\frac{1}{2}$" of material at the bottom edge of the aprons. This will help you position the piece in the right location and also adds

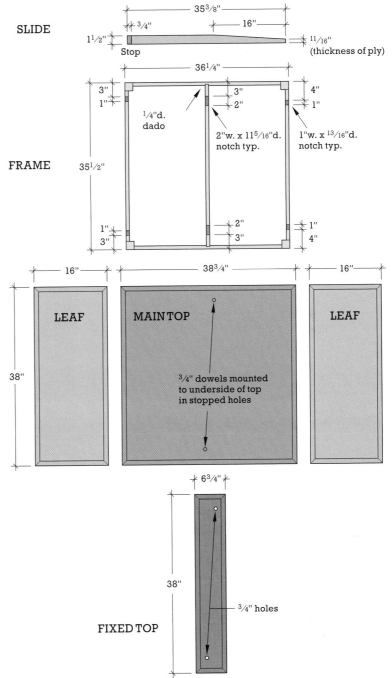

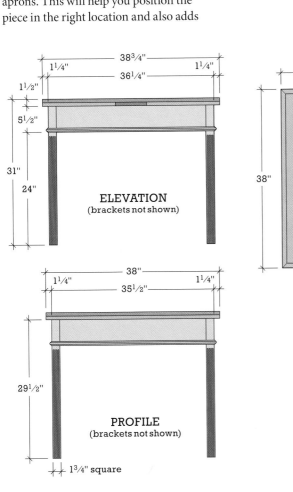

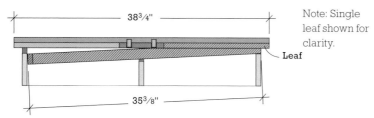

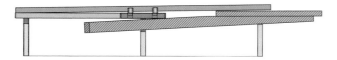

In closed position, extension leaf with attached slide is fully housed beneath floating main top.

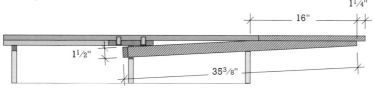

As extension leaf is pulled outward, floating main top pivots upward. Main top is held in alignment with base by attached dowels that ride in holes in narrow fixed top.

1 1/4"

16"

1 1/2"

35 3/8"

When extension leaf is fully extended, it is flush with floating main top. Main top returns to rest on beveled edge of slide. Stop block, attached to side of slide, contacts center support and prevents overextension.

strength by adding support beneath the piece. Square the dado with a chisel to finish.

Now you are ready for some assembly. Add glue into the mortises and on the tenons and slip the joint together. Assemble the base in steps, but remember that your mortises open into each other and the glue can run out the opposite mortise. Allow one set of rails and aprons to dry, then complete the assembly with the other set. Finally, slide the center support into the aprons and attach.

Continuous Grain Tops it Off

Cut the pieces for your top, leaves and the fixed top from a single sheet of plywood. It will look best if you make the grain of the leaves continuous with the main top. Rip the sheet to 36" in width, and then cut (in this order) one leaf, the main top and the second leaf. This will allow you to arrange the pieces so that when the table is fully extended, the grain will run the entire length of the table. Don't forget

Layout is the key to the slides and the tapers. First, make a regular pass at the jointer, stopping as the cut reaches the 8"-layout line.

Second, reverse the cut and "wheelie" down the area of the first cut while passing the piece over the knives. The cut will not make contact until the 16" line, and will taper the cut the final dimensions.

Dowel

Fixed top   Stop block

The 2 1/4"-long dowels extend down from the top and through the fixed top. The stop blocks at the ends of each slide need to be removable in order to disassemble and finish the table.

Set the depth stop at the drill press to leave 3/4" and drill the 5/8"-diameter holes into the tapered portion of the slides. Use a tapered countersink centered at each hole to attach the slides to the leaves with #8 × 1 1/4" screws.

Supplies

Woodworker's Supply
woodworker.com or 800-645-9292

4 oz. • J.E. Moser's Early American
Cherry water-soluble aniline
dye, item #844-624, $28.99

Price as of publication date.

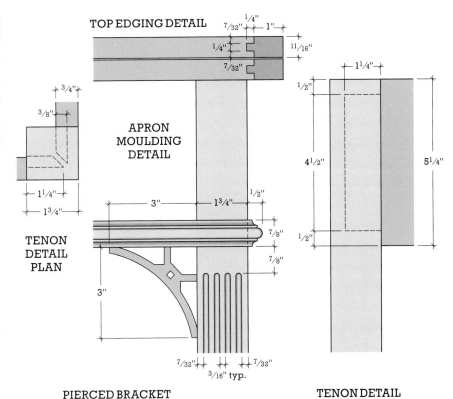

TOP EDGING DETAIL

APRON
MOULDING
DETAIL

TENON
DETAIL
PLAN

PIERCED BRACKET
DETAIL

TENON DETAIL
ELEVATION

to cut the fixed top, while you're at it.

Now we need to add the solid-wood edging to the plywood. I elected to run a simple tongue and groove to improve the joint. Use a router bit with a three-wing cutter (eagleamerica.com or 800-872-2511, item #199-4622) to make the ¼"-deep groove in the plywood. To ensure that the groove is centered, I like to make a complete pass from both faces of the plywood.

Create the tongues on the solid stock edging pieces in a series of two-step rabbet cuts on the table saw. Make sure to check the fit. Because I ran the groove cut from both faces, it is likely that the groove will be more than the ¼"-wide, and you want a snug fit for your table edging. To make things easier, I ran my edging more than double the needed width, then ran the tongues on both edges. I then rip those pieces to the finished size for the edging. I use a 1" finished size (1¼" including the tongue) because it takes the guesswork out of sizing the top plywood pieces.

Carefully fit the edging around the plywood panels, mitering the corners. Slide the edging into the grooves and match the corners of the two pieces. Hold them in position and mark the opposite miter length at the exact corner. Repeat these steps for all four sides of the panels and for all four panels.

Miter the corners of the moulding and use a thin bead of glue. Too much glue and the result might squeeze out onto the aprons, causing finish problems.

Locate the first bracket for the square hole and mark the edges on the scrap below in order to position the remaining brackets for this step.

With one pierced bracket complete, fit a scrap into the ¼" hole to locate the position for the remaining brackets. Transfer the design onto the remaining pieces.

The pierced brackets fit into the corners where the aprons meet the legs. Use a small amount of glue and ⅛"-diameter dowels to secure.

Tailored Tea Table

BY GLEN D. HUEY

In Colonial America, prior to Paul Revere's famous midnight ride, colonists adopted many of the lifestyles of English citizens. One such behavior was afternoon tea. Of course, you couldn't be of a wealthy class and partake in tea without having the necessary serving implements – including a tea table.

Tea tables came into vogue in the early 1700s and were built in many designs such as tray-topped, round-topped and porringer-topped tables with either carved cabriole legs or turned cabriole legs. A tray-topped design with carved legs was by far the most high-end table one could possess.

After the tea party in Boston, the idea of afternoon tea all but disappeared in the American colonies, but the furniture design survives to this day.

Cabrioles Without a Lathe

Queen Anne-style furniture makers focus on curves and achieving a light, graceful look. Cabriole legs are all about curves, and to give a lighter look to the design, slipper feet were the choice for many tea tables.

Forget the lathe. A slipper foot is

shaped by hand. To begin work on the legs, copy the pattern from the drawings on page 22. Next, transfer the shape to a piece of hardboard or thin plywood. Each leg requires you to trace the pattern onto two adjacent sides of each leg blank. Transferring from paper would be tedious. Mill the leg stock to size and trace the pattern to the stock.

At the band saw you'll need to cut to the lines. Freehand cutting is the only option, but there are a few tips to make the task easier. Starting with one face, begin cutting on a straight section of the leg. Cut halfway, then carefully back the blade out of the cut. Cut the balance of that profile entering from the opposite direction, but stop prior to reaching the previous cut. That creates a bridge that holds the waste material in place so the leg pattern remains on the second face. If the blade shows signs of being pinched as you back out of that cut, squeeze the leg at the straight cut to allow ample room for extraction.

Complete the band saw work on the remaining lines for the first face of the leg. On the second face there's no need for a bridge, so saw away until the parts fall free.

Then it's back to the first face to break down the bridge. When the cuts are all completed, you have a square-shaped leg that is in need of shaping.

From Round to Square

Shaping the legs looks more intimidating than it is. Start at the ankle and make that area completely round. To guide me, I use a pattern that's made with a 1" drill bit. Drill a hole in a plywood or hardboard scrap then split the hole down the center. The resulting half-circle is used as a template for rounding the ankle, as shown on page 22.

Next, shape each leg from round at the ankle to square at the knee. Work one leg at a time, shaping each edge from bottom to top. The transition is gradual. Use your hands to feel the shape. A Shinto rasp is my tool of choice for shaping legs. I like the aggressiveness of the tool when

roughing out the profile.

Smooth the leg with the second side of the Shinto or other rasp but save the finish sanding until the foot area and above the knee is shaped.

Shaping a Slipper

Shaping the leg is a rather quick task. But, the work on the individual feet is where the majority of shaping time is spent. Begin shaping the foot by drawing an "X" on each foot's bottom. Next, make a pattern of the foot from the drawings just as you did for the leg. Center the pattern on the foot bottom with the point matching the front corner of the leg. (See bottom-left photo on page 23.) Trace the pattern onto each foot.

Use a combination square to draw 45°-angle lines across the foot, parallel to the pattern. Extend those lines up the sides of each foot then saw away the waste material. The lines on the sides guide your sawing to keep from wasting needed material. It's easy to cut too close to the ankles.

Shape the foot to the pattern, making sure you keep the sides of the foot perpendicular to the foot's bottom. Pay

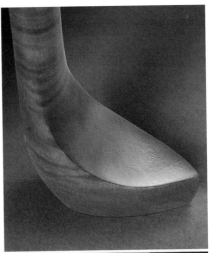

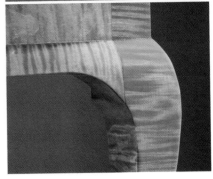

Mundane becomes exceptional with the addition of slipper feet, graceful curves and intricate details and craftsmanship.

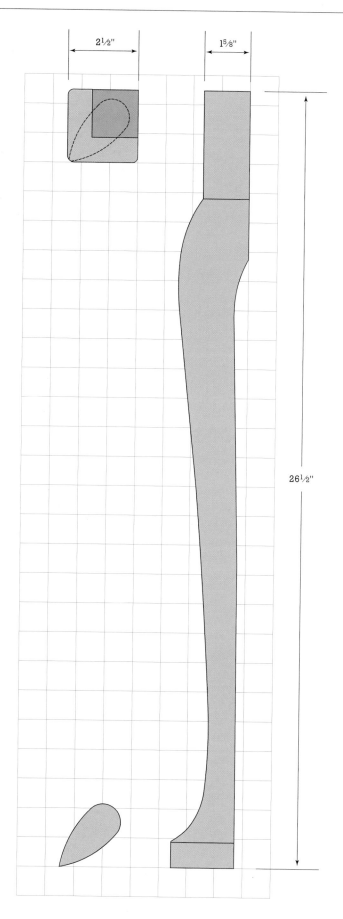

2½"   1⅝"

26½"

FOOT & LEG PATTERNS
Each square = 1"

If you begin the leg layout work with the stock milled to size, it doesn't matter whether you match the knees or the heels when tracing your patterns.

particular attention to the rear of the foot. The heel has to roll down and blend in with the foot's shape.

Finish shaping the foot by drawing a matching profile ⅛" inside the foot bottom. Each side of the foot is then beveled slightly to that profile. The heel continues to roll to the inside line.

Shaping the top of the foot is the next task. Using hand tools for this is real work. The simplest method I've found is to use a spindle sander. Install a 3" drum with a coarse-grit sleeve on the sander, then slowly sculpt the top of the foot. The idea is to level the foot's top and make a gradual transition to the ankle. Check your progress often. As you get near the ankle, begin to slowly rotate the leg and form the beginnings of the roundness that transitions to the full-round ankle.

Once the shaping of the leg and foot is completed, move to the band saw to remove the waste material from the top block. There is a certain order in which to make this cut. The first cut is with the knee positioned facing the saw's table. To make the second cut simply rotate the leg 90° so one face of the knee is facing up. Following this procedure allows the leg to be fully supported as you cut.

Shape the knee, as well as the area above the knee, then sand the entire leg with #150-grit sanding discs. At this time

A simple shop-made jig is the perfect tool for defining the shape of the ankle of a cabriole leg. This slim tea-table ankle is 1".

stand the legs side by side and look for any variations in shape. This is the time to fine-tune the legs so they match. But, don't get carried away with this task. Remember: The legs stand 17" apart at minimum. Slight variations will be imperceptible in the finished table.

Profile & Fit the Aprons

Aprons join the legs with mortise-and-tenon joints. Positioning the legs to cut a mortise in the correct location is a bit tricky. Place a support under the top block of the leg to keep the knee off the surface. As you can see in the bottom-left photo on page 25, I cut the $1/4" \times 4^3/4" \times 1"$ mortises with the back of the leg block against the fence of a dedicated mortise machine.

Aprons are cut to size according to the cut list on page 24 and tenons are formed on both ends of each apron to fit the mortises. Before assembly takes place, slot openings for the candle slides have to be cut into the end aprons. Locate the slot, then use a plunge router with a $5/8"$ straight bit to create the opening. A straight fence attached to the router makes this quick work. Chisel the corners square, then begin work on the inside face of the apron.

On the inside of each end apron there are two $3/4" \times 2^1/8" \times 1/4"$-deep dados that capture the candle-slide supports. The supports are held down from the top edge of the aprons $3/8"$ to accommodate the recessed top and are press-fit into the candle-slide openings. A straight fence and $3/4"$ pattern bit work great to make the dados. Again, square the corners with your chisel.

Sand the aprons through #150 grit then fit one apron to a mating leg. Hold the apron flush with the top edge of the leg, then draw a pattern on the lower apron edge so the rounded profile of the knee bracket area continues onto the apron as in the top-left photo on page 26. (A 5" sanding disc makes a perfect pattern.)

Blend the radius of the pattern up $1^1/16"$ on the apron. Repeat the pattern on both ends of each apron then make the cuts at the band saw. Smooth the edges with light sanding at a spindle sander.

Now it's time to assemble the base of the table. It's best to assemble the base in two steps. First, glue the side aprons to the legs. After the glue is set, assemble the end aprons to the legs. Add glue to both the mortises and tenons, then slip the joints together, making sure to keep the top edges flush. Allow the glue to dry, then sand the entire workpiece to #180 grit. You'll have to touch up the sanding later during the project, but this is the best time to do the majority of the work.

Next, you'll need to create small slots for the wooden clips used to secure the top. A couple options for cutting the slots are a router or router table with a $1/4"$ slot-cutting router bit (the tea table is light and compact enough to hoist onto your router table), or use a biscuit joiner and complete the slot in two overlapping cuts.

Position the slots from $1/2"$ to $3/4"$ down

Transfer the foot pattern to hardboard to make repeated layout easy. If you start shaping with a matching pattern, the end results should match as well.

The majority of the waste in shaping the slipper foot is removed with a saw. It's important to plan the layout lines and cut to those lines. Deviations could alter the foot shape.

The edges of the feet taper $1/8"$ while the heel continues to roll to the floor. Draw the inner profile freehand.

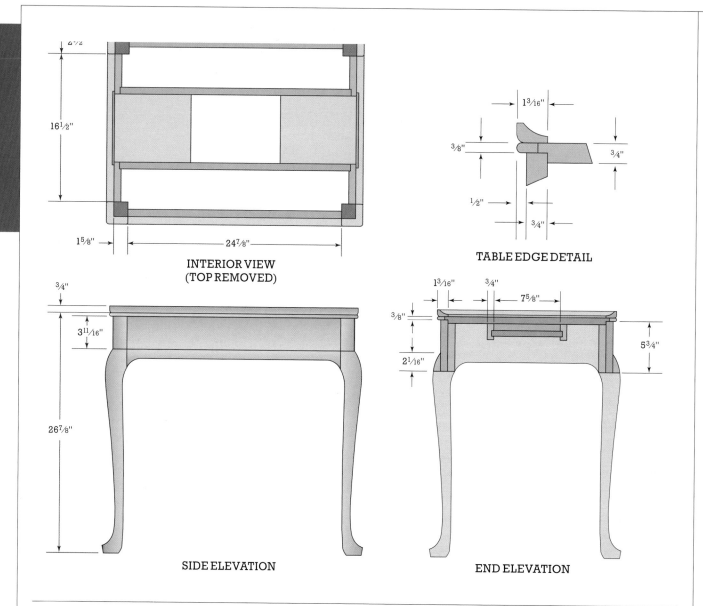

**INTERIOR VIEW
(TOP REMOVED)**

TABLE EDGE DETAIL

SIDE ELEVATION

END ELEVATION

Tailored Tea Table

NO.	ITEM	DIMENSIONS (INCHES)			MATERIAL	COMMENTS
		T	W	L		
4	Legs	$2^1/_2$	$2^1/_2$	$26^1/_2$	Tiger maple	
2	End aprons	$3/_4$	$5^3/_4$	$18^1/_2$	Tiger maple	1" tenon, both ends
2	Side aprons	$3/_4$	$5^3/_4$	$26^7/_8$	Tiger maple	1" tenon, both ends
1	Top	$3/_4$	$18^3/_4$	$26^{15}/_{16}$	Tiger maple	
8	Wooden clips	$3/_4$	$7/_8$	$2^1/_2$	Tiger maple/poplar	
Knee Return Brackets						
2	End brackets	$3/_4$	$2^1/_8$	$16^1/_2$	Tiger maple	
2	Side brackets	$3/_4$	$2^1/_8$	$24^7/_8$	Tiger maple	
Candle Slide Parts						
2	Supports	$3/_4$	$1^3/_4$	$26^3/_4$	Poplar	
2	Candle slides	$9/_{16}$	$8^1/_4$	8	Tiger maple	
2	Candle-slide fronts	$1/_4$	$7/_8$	$8^1/_2$	Tiger maple	
Tray Moulding Parts						
2	Long beads	$3/_8$	$7/_8$	$29^1/_8$	Tiger maple	
2	Short beads	$3/_8$	$7/_8$	$20^3/_4$	Tiger maple	
1	Long cove	$3/_4$	$2^1/_2$	32	Tiger maple	Becomes 2 pcs.
1	Short cove	$3/_4$	$2^1/_2$	23	Tiger maple	Becomes 2 pcs.

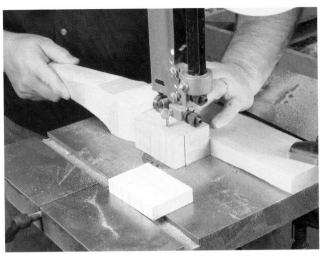

Hand tools can achieve a flat foot top, but power sanding at a spindle sander is quick, accurate and repeatable. Goodbye hard-to-work end grain.

There is a specific cut order to remove the waste from the two faces of the leg block. Choose wisely and the work is quick.

from the top edge of the aprons. With the slots located in this position, the tongue of each wooden clip is set toward the middle (see page 28). If you slide any further down the apron, you'll likely cut into the candle-slide opening in the end aprons.

Shaped Knee-Return Brackets

Another feature that adds interest to the design of this tea table is the shaped knee-return brackets. On most carved cabriole-legged furniture, the knee returns extend to or slightly over the aprons or other rails. However, on some tea tables the brackets extend from leg to leg, adding shape and shadow lines.

Begin with blanks that fit snug between the knees of the legs. Draw pencil lines along the leg curvature to transfer the shape to the returns. Also, transfer the design from the bottom edge of the aprons onto the returns.

Angle the table saw blade then position the fence to remove as much waste as possible.

The flat surface on the face of the returns is enough to hold the pieces flat at the band saw to cut the apron-matching design. But, if you make a continuous cut, the flat area is removed and the piece becomes unsteady. It's best to make the cut in sections to leave short portions of flat area intact. This allows you to maintain control throughout the cut.

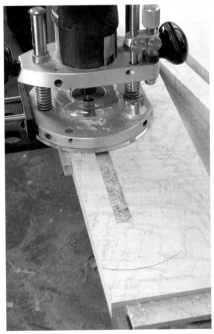

To cut the mortises into the legs, you need to add support under the top block so the knee is off the table. Add a small wedge below the knee to stabilize the piece.

A plunge router and straight bit make quick work of cutting the candle-slide opening. Of course, an attached fence is a must-have.

Routing the dado for the candle-slide supports is a snap. Use a pattern bit with a straight fence that you set right on the layout line.

It takes time to set up a compass or trammel to lay out the curve necessary for the transition from knee to apron. Shop items such as this sanding disc do the job – and are usually right at hand.

Bevel the table saw blade to remove as much waste as possible from the knee returns without cutting into the profile portion.

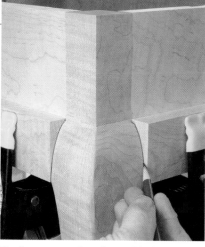

The knee-return brackets add visual interest to the overall design. Once the proper thickness is achieved, transfer the profile and begin to shape the returns.

Use a spindle sander or drum sander at the drill press to smooth to the lines. Again, the flat areas help maintain control. Once the edges are smooth flip the piece and, using a pencil or marking knife, connect the straight portions to provide a line to remove the balance of the waste material. Use the band saw to remove the final waste material then sand those areas; the return brackets are now ready for final shaping to the leg profile.

Final shaping is done with a small handplane. Work the profile to match the leg area, then finish smoothing with rasps and by sanding. Finish sand the returns to #180 grit.

The brackets are glued to the lower edge of the aprons – no fasteners are needed. To keep the glue from squeezing out above the bracket where it would be difficult to remove, make a shallow table saw cut just below the top edge of the

bracket on the back face. That cut acts as a reservoir for excess glue. Add a thin bead of glue to the bracket below the cut then position the brackets to the apron. Add a few spring clamps until the glue is set.

Adding the Candle Slides

While the glue sets, cut and fit the candle-slide supports. Fit the pieces to the base then mark the exact location of the slide opening. Cut a $5/8$" × $1/4$" × 10" groove at each opening.

A straight bit and a router table are your best bet for this task. Align the layout marks with the router bit, set the fence and create the groove. Setting a stop for the length of cut allows easy removal of the support after the groove is cut. The supports are held in place with a bit of glue where the bottom of the slide fits the dado in the end aprons.

Next, make the candle slides so they fit the opening. Mill the material, making sure to orient the grain across the opening. Then create the front piece for each slide with all edges profiled with a $1/4$" roundover router bit.

Mill this profile on wide stock, then slice the fronts at the table saw. This eliminates working with small pieces. Run the four edges to create a $1/16$" shadow line on the profile (as you would when profiling drawer fronts), then rip

To keep the stock level throughout the cut, leave tabs on the knee-return brackets. Create a tab as you reach the end of the band saw table. The tabs are later removed with the stock positioned face up.

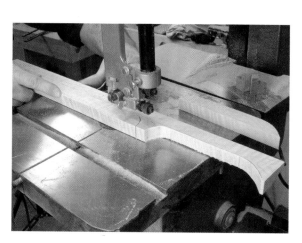

The best way to shape the knee-return brackets is with a small handplane. Watch the grain direction and the results should be near finish-ready.

With the opening for the candle slides transferred to the support, locating the cutting position of the matching router bit is all that's needed to create the groove. Turn the carbide cutter perpendicular to the fence to set up the cut.

Profile the edges of the candle-slide fronts on a larger piece of stock, then rip the individual pieces to size. At no time do my fingers get close to the blade.

To keep from marring the fronts of the slides, use tape and a small bead of glue. The tape acts as a clamp until the glue sets.

the fronts off. A zero-clearance insert keeps the moulded piece from dropping into the saw.

Finish sand the candle-slide parts to #180 grit and prepare to attach the fronts to the slides. Align the fronts with a ¼" above the slide and equal distance to each side. Again, a small amount of glue does the job. Add a thin bead of glue, position the fronts to the slides then use tape to hold the connection until the glue has dried. Use small brass screws as stops to keep the slides from being pulled from the base. Those stops are applied after finishing is complete.

Beginning the Tray Mouldings
In order to properly size the top, you'll need to build the first layer of tray moulding, which is the beaded frame. The overhang of the completed frame is ½" all around. Prepare the four pieces of stock then rout the edge profile with a ⅜" bead-forming router bit.

The beaded frame is joined at the corners with half-lapped joinery. Make the necessary cuts at the table saw and keep in mind the orientation of the profiled edge. It's easy to remove the incorrect

With the bead-frame stock at ⅜", it has plenty of rigidity to shape at a router table. There's no need to rip profiled moulding from wider boards.

Cut the half-lap joinery on the bead frame using the table saw and a miter gauge. Pushing the stock back and forth across the blade creates a smooth level surface.

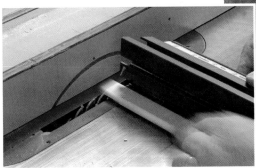

The bead frame is the first layer of moulding. It's joined at the corners with half-lap joinery and captures the recessed top.

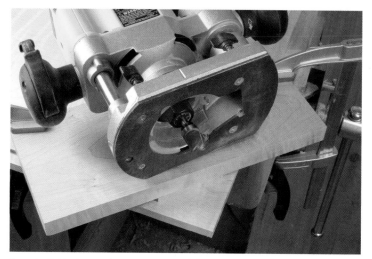

Any straightedge and a pattern router bit, in this case a $5/8$"-diameter bit, produces a clean cut at the top corners to allow for the recessed top to fit in position.

Supplies

Horton Brasses Inc.
horton-brasses.com or 800-754-9127
2 • brass desk interior knobs, $1/2$", item #H-42, $3.50–$4.20 ea.
Price as of publication date.

portion of the joint.

I found it best to create the bead then round the corners at the joints after assembly versus joining the frame and moulding it afterward. This allows you more control working with thin stock.

Assemble the frame with glue. Small F-style clamps apply pressure to hold the corners tight. You need to check the assembly for square as you walk through the glue-up. Once the glue is dry, make sure the overhang is correct, then use a thin bead of glue and 23-gauge pins to attach the frame to the table base.

Free-Floating Tabletop

Because this table has mouldings in a cross-grain relationship to the top, I elected to attach the tray mouldings to the top edge of the base and allow the top itself to float. With the bead frame in

place, fit and install the top.

Mill the top to size and thickness, then fit the top inside the bead frame. Because wood moves across the grain, you'll need to take into consideration what season of the year you're building the piece. Allow $1/8$" if you're in low-humidity times to almost no gap if you're building with humidity on the high side. As for the length of the top, wood doesn't move much with the grain, so I fit that area snug.

The top is rabbeted along all sides to fit flush with the bead frame. I use a two-step rabbeting method at the table saw, but there are many ways to cut rabbets. Select the method that works best for you.

Whatever method you choose, there is one additional step necessary before the top is attached to the base. You need to

remove material at the corners of the top that correspond with the leg posts. Use a straightedge and flush-cut router bit to remove the waste.

With the milling of the top complete, sand the piece to #180 grit, add a drop of glue to the exact center of the end aprons, then position the top to the base. The glue adds extra hold to the top, forcing any movement outward to the sides and divides overall wood movement in half. Each half acts independently.

Add the wooden clips to the base and installation of the top is complete. The clips are made at the table saw, counterbored for screws, then installed with #8 × $1 1/4$" woodscrews. The clips allow the top to move, but keep it tight to the base.

Creating the Tray's Cove Moulding

The tray's cove mouldings begin as two pieces of flat stock milled to $3/4$" thick. Next you'll need to produce a cove cut centered on the stock that results in the correct end measurements for the cove once the stock is ripped into two matching pieces.

At the table saw, with the blade height adjusted to $1/2$", position an auxiliary fence for the cut. Twisting the fence manipulates the cut, so it's necessary to find the exact setup position. I take two pieces of stock and draw my cove profile on opposing ends. Position the drawn profile toward the blade and maneuver the auxiliary fence until the infeed and outfeed of the blade align with the layout marks. Once found, lock the position of the fence.

The top-left photo on the next page shows the setup at the table saw. I like my auxiliary fence on the outfeed side of the blade, and I've secured the stock in position with a magnetic fence to keep the moulding from moving.

Lower the blade then make successive cuts, each time raising the blade

A top with movement. Wooden clips hold the floating top to the table base and allow for seasonal movement. This relieves any cross-grain construction concerns.

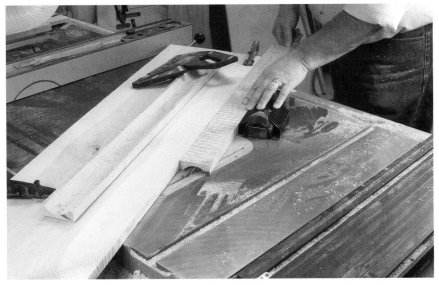

This is the setup used to create cove mouldings. With the fence above the blade, you're responsible for holding the stock tight to the fence. A featherboard helps with that task.

Ready to miter. The tray cove moulding is created as a single cove moulding then split exactly at the center to provide twice the length.

incrementally to produce a cove profile matching the desired design. Take the last pass very slowly in order to remove as many mill marks as possible, which will reduce the amount of sanding.

Finish sand the tray cove mouldings to #180 grit then use a table saw to split the stock in half, forming two identical strips per piece. Each piece is routed with a ³⁄₈" roundover bit on the bottom edge to reflect the edge treatment of the profile of the bead frame below. Finish sand any rough areas before fitting the moulding to the table.

Those mouldings are attached to the table with brads located so the top is free to move. The brads extend through the cove moulding and the bead frame into the aprons. Fit each piece of moulding in place, then temporarily attach it to the table with one 23-gauge pin at each end. When the task is complete, the mouldings and pins are easily removed.

Clean up pencil lines. Add a thin bead of glue to the cove, position the mouldings to the table and attach them with brads – the square holes left from the brad gun mimic antique, square-head nails.

To secure the coved corners, peg each miter with a short length of ¹⁄₈" dowel.

Race to the Finish

For the finish I elected to stain the piece with water-base aniline dye stain (a 50-50 mixture of golden amber maple and brown walnut), add a single coat of boiled linseed oil to highlight the stripes, then topcoat with a few layers of shellac.

Normally I would rub out the shellac to achieve a dull sheen. To save time and effort, I elected to spray a single coat of dull-rubbed-effect lacquer to achieve that sheen. If you don't spray your finish, try wiping on a coat of satin polyurethane or wiping varnish.

Add the brass knobs and brass screw stops to the candle slides and you're ready to sit down for an enjoyable afternoon of tea – or coffee, if you just haven't been able to get over that entire taxation-without-representation mess.

Prep work saves patience. Half the battle in fitting the tray cove is determining where the cut lines are located. Lay out 45° lines that bisect the corners, then cut to those lines.

Shaker Trestle Table

BY GLEN D. HUEY

Nibbling away the mortise locations on the leg halves can be accomplished with a flat-tooth rip blade or a dado stack.

I've built a number of trestle tables in the Shaker style over the years, usually following the style of an original table from one Shaker collection or another. But when I decided to do a trestle table for *Popular Woodworking* readers, I took a second look at some of the designs and decided I could add a feature and come up with a stronger table without sacrificing the simple Shaker lines.

The one shown here is a standard two-pedestal table with a single stretcher tying the bases together. One of the concerns I've always had with this design was the stability of the joint at the stretcher. Anyone who has been to a family dinner at my house knows that a sturdy table is important when everyone starts hungrily reaching for platters of food. To solve the stability concern I doubled-up the hardware from another sturdy piece of furniture – the bed. By using a pair of bed bolts at each joint, this table becomes amazingly stout.

Save Money on Wood

If you've seen my other furniture, you know I'm addicted to figured maple. Though they've tried to get me into treatment, I haven't yet accepted that I have a problem.

But when it came to choosing the wood for this table, even I had to admit that with such a simple piece, adding busy figure to the base would be gilding

the lily. So I saved the good stuff for the top and chose to use painted poplar to build the base.

Half a Foot, not Six Inches

Construction on the base begins with the feet blanks. The feet actually are two "half-feet" that you face-glue together. This allows you to conserve lumber (no sense trying to find 3" × 3" wood for a painted base) and you can make the mortise for the leg post before gluing the halves together. Mill out the two halves for each foot, then clamp the pairs together and lay out the two notches that will form the $1\frac{1}{2}" \times 2\frac{1}{4}"$ mortise for the post tenon.

There are many ways to remove the waste material from the notches, but I'm a table-saw guy, so that's where I headed. Use your miter gauge and make repeated passes across the blade to nibble away the waste area on all four pieces, as shown above.

With the notches cut, it's time to make the halves a whole. When gluing the two halves together, the last thing you want are the pieces to "creep," or slide on the glue, which will cause misalignment. My solution is to mount a 1" section of a #6 finish nail into one half by drilling a small hole and gluing in the nail piece with the point out. As you glue the two halves, align the two sections and press them together. The nails "bite" into the wood and prevent creeping. Go ahead

and clamp the pieces securely and set them aside to dry.

While the feet could be left flat at the floor, it's not as attractive as shaping them to leave "pads" at either end. It also helps the table to sit flat on uneven floors. To form the pads, clamp the two assembled feet together with the bottoms facing the same direction. Mark the pads on the feet according to the illustrations, then drill a $\frac{3}{8}$" hole at the transition point at either end. The hole itself will create the small radius for the transition. After making the two holes per foot, head to the band saw to cut away the portion between the radius cuts to finish the pad shapes.

Some simple shaping using a couple of saws will give the feet an even more graceful look. First cut a 7° bevel on the ends of the feet using the table saw. Next, make a mark $\frac{3}{4}$" down from the top edge at the ends of each foot. Make another mark $10\frac{1}{2}$" in toward the mortise at the top of the leg. Connect the two marks and you have the slope for the top of each foot. Head to the band saw and cut the slopes. To finish the feet, sand the surfaces and round all the edges with a $\frac{3}{16}$" radius bit in your router.

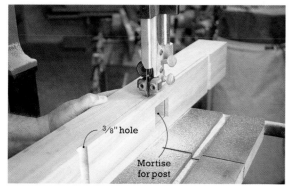

After gluing the halves together, I first drilled two $3/8$" holes to define the foot pad and then connected the dots. The rest was simple band saw work.

With the post cut to shape, the first step in forming the tenon is to define the shoulder on all four sides. The miter gauge (hidden behind the work) on my saw works well, while the rip fence allows you to set the shoulder location.

Going Vertical

The next step is the $2^7/8$" × $2^7/8$" posts. As with the feet, there's a good chance you'll need to glue up thinner pieces to form the posts.

Once assembled and milled to the size given in the cutting list, it's time to form the tenons to match the mortises in the feet. Start cutting the tenons by first defining the shoulder on the table saw with the posts flat on the saw's table. Then reset the table saw and run the posts upright to form the cheeks. Cut two cheeks, then adjust the fence and cut the other two. Make the tenons slightly oversize and then trim them to achieve a snug fit.

At the tops of the posts, cut out a notch the width of the post to hold the cross braces. Lay out this notch using the photos above to locate them. Note that the notches aren't centered in the posts – rather, they're offset by $1/4$" to one side. An easy method to remove the 4" of waste is to hog the majority out with a band saw, then chisel away the remain-

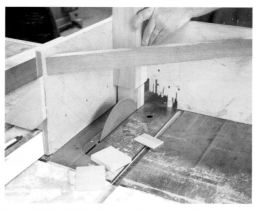

I use a high-sided shop-made tenoning jig to cut the cheeks on the tenon. You could also nibble away the waste á la the foot mortise if you don't have, or want to build, a tenoning jig.

The top of the post is notched 4" deep, so the table saw won't cut it (pun intended). The band saw will and I use staggered cuts to remove much of the wood, then chisel out the excess. Notice the notch isn't centered on the post, but offset by $1/4$" to one side.

ing waste. To finish off the posts, use a chamfer bit in your router to make decorative cuts on each edge, stopping $7/8$" from the joinery at each end.

Visible Means of Support

The part of the leg that actually supports the top is the cross brace. Mill the stock

for the cross braces, then use the table saw to nibble away the shallow notches (as you did on the feet halves) on the two opposing sides of each brace. These notches will fit into the 4"-deep notches at the tops of the leg posts, so test the fit to make sure it's snug, but not too tight.

While the cross braces are mostly hid-

Shaker Trestle Table

NO.	ITEM	DIMENSIONS (INCHES)			MATERIAL
		T	W	L	
4	Feet halves	$1^{11}/16$	3	30	Poplar
2	Cross braces	$1^1/2$	4	30	Poplar
2	Posts	$2^7/8$	$2^7/8$	$29^3/8$	Poplar
1	Center brace	$1^1/2$	2	28	Poplar
1	Stretcher	$1^1/2$	6	$43^1/4$	Poplar
1	Top	$7/8$	36	71	Cherry
2	Breadboard ends	$7/8$	$1^1/2$	38*	Cherry
10	Top fasteners	$3/4$	$7/8$	$2^1/4$	Cherry
*Finished size is 36" long.					

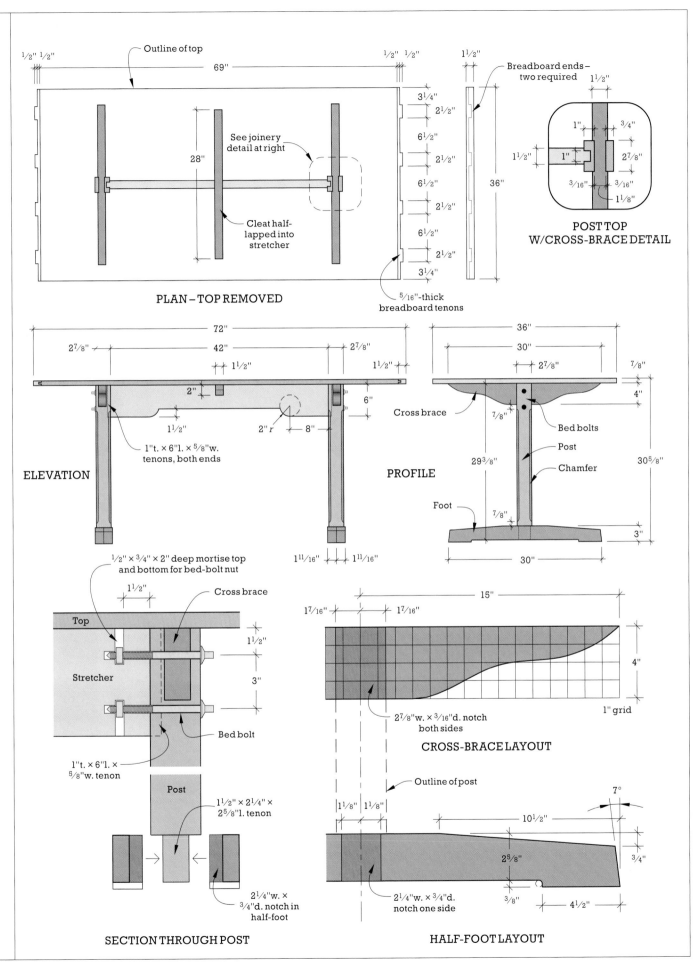

PLAN – TOP REMOVED

Outline of top

69"

See joinery detail at right

28"

Cleat half-lapped into stretcher

¹⁄₂" ¹⁄₂"

¹⁄₂" ¹⁄₂"

3¹⁄₄"
2¹⁄₂"
6¹⁄₂"
2¹⁄₂"
6¹⁄₂"
2¹⁄₂"
6¹⁄₂"
2¹⁄₂"
3¹⁄₄"

⁵⁄₁₆"-thick breadboard tenons

Breadboard ends– two required

1¹⁄₂"
1¹⁄₂"
36"

POST TOP W/CROSS-BRACE DETAIL

1"
³⁄₄"
1¹⁄₂"
1"
2⁷⁄₈"
³⁄₁₆"
³⁄₁₆"
1¹⁄₈"

ELEVATION

72"
2⁷⁄₈"
42"
2⁷⁄₈"
1¹⁄₂"
1¹⁄₂"
2"
6"
1¹⁄₂"
2"r
8"
1"t. × 6"l. × ⁵⁄₈"w. tenons, both ends
1¹¹⁄₁₆"
1¹¹⁄₁₆"

PROFILE

36"
30"
2⁷⁄₈"
⁷⁄₈"
4"
Cross brace
⁷⁄₈"
Bed bolts
Post
Chamfer
29³⁄₈"
30⁵⁄₈"
Foot
⁷⁄₈"
3"
30"

SECTION THROUGH POST

¹⁄₂" × ³⁄₄" × 2" deep mortise top and bottom for bed-bolt nut
1¹⁄₂"
Cross brace
Top
1¹⁄₂"
Stretcher
3"
Bed bolt
1"t. × 6"l. × ⁵⁄₈"w. tenon
Post
1¹⁄₂" × 2¹⁄₄" × 2⁵⁄₈"l. tenon
2¹⁄₄"w. × ³⁄₄"d. notch in half-foot

CROSS-BRACE LAYOUT

15"
1⁷⁄₁₆"
1⁷⁄₁₆"
4"
1" grid
2⁷⁄₈"w. × ³⁄₁₆"d. notch both sides

HALF-FOOT LAYOUT

Outline of post
1¹⁄₈"
1¹⁄₈"
7°
10¹⁄₂"
2⁵⁄₈"
³⁄₄"
2¹⁄₄"w. × ³⁄₄"d. notch one side
³⁄₈"
4¹⁄₂"

den under the tabletop, they can be seen at times and therefore there's no sense leaving them square and chunky. Use the pattern (on page 33) to trace or mark the curved shape on the pieces themselves. Then use the band saw to cut out the shape on the braces, cutting wide of the line and then smoothing the curve with sandpaper.

Now glue the foot and cross brace to each post. To add a bit more strength after the glue has dried, drill two $7/16$" holes (on opposite sides of the leg) in each joint and pin the joint with dowels. Make sure to stagger the pins on each side so they don't run into each other. Using a knife or sandpaper, taper one end of each peg a bit to make it easier to insert in its hole. After tapping the dowels in place, cut the extra length nearly flush to the leg surface and sand it smooth.

Bridging the Gap

With the ends assembled it's time to attach the stretcher to tie everything together. This is the joint where you need all the strength you can muster. As I mentioned earlier, I used bed bolts here, but I started with the traditional method of cutting mortises in the legs and tenons on both ends of the stretcher. Start by cutting the $1" \times 6"$-long $\times 5/8"$-deep mortises on the thicker side of each assembly. I used a Forstner bit to make most of the mortise (see below) then chiseled out the waste to square everything up, but you could use a router with a straight bit. To create the short tenons on the stretcher, I used a rabbeting bit in a router to cut rabbets on opposite faces of the stretcher.

If you haven't used bed bolts before, they're essentially heavy-duty bolts that screw into a square nut buried in a mortise in the other piece. After cutting the rabbets on the stretcher, make two $1/2"$ $\times 3/4" \times 2"$-deep mortises at each end of

the stretcher, one in the top edge and one in the bottom edge, to hold the bed-bolt nuts.

To add more stability to the table, a third center brace is half-lapped into the center top of the stretcher. Mill the stock for this part and use one of the finished cross braces as a pattern to shape the center brace. Next, use the illustration to lay out the decorative cut on the bottom edge of the stretcher. Then use the table saw and miter gauge to cut the half-lap joint for the center brace. This piece is attached with glue and a 2" wood screw, but don't attach it until you're done installing the bed bolts.

Use a drill press to make the holes in the trestle legs for the bed bolts. The holes are $7/16"$ in diameter and are in the center of the stretcher mortises, $1 1/2"$ from both the top edge and bottom edge of the mortise. To finish making the hole for the bed bolt, slip a stretcher tenon into the end section, clamping the two

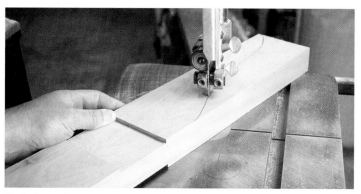

Sculpting a shape on the cross braces isn't necessary to keep the table sturdy, but it does keep it from looking clunky. After transferring the pattern onto the brace, I cut wide of the line on the band saw, then used a spindle sander to smooth the shape.

With the cross braces glued to the posts, they are pegged in position. Clamp them tight and check for square between the post and brace. Note that the pegs are at opposite corners of the joint. This allows room for the mortise (in the next step).

Here's the mortise for the stretcher. I removed most of the waste with a Forstner bit, then chiseled the mortise square.

Getting the holes for the bed bolts straight is important. And the best tool for that task is the drill press. The two $7/16"$ holes are located in $1 1/2"$ from the top and bottom edges of the mortise.

pieces firmly. Use a long $7/16$" drill bit to finish the hole through the end of the stretcher and into the mortise area created for the bed-bolt nut. The straight hole at the drill press acts as a guide to drill the remainder of the hole straight. Clean out any waste from the hole, place the nuts into the mortises, slide the bolt into the hole, and attach it to the nut. Tighten the connection with a wrench.

Holding the Top in Place

I use wooden clips to hold the top in place on the base. The clips have a rabbet cut on one end that slips into slots cut into the cross braces on the base. I use a biscuit cutter set to make a cut for a #20 biscuit and start the slot $1/2$" down from the top of the brace. Because the tenon on the clip is almost $1/4$" thick, make two cuts with the biscuit joiner, lowering the cutter to finish the cut at $1/4$" wide. Place two slots on each inside of the cross braces and one on either side of the center brace.

Rather than trying to cut rabbets on the ends of the little wooden clips, start with a 5"-6" wide piece of wood that is $4 5/8$" long and $3/4$" thick. Cut a $1/2$" × $1/2$" rabbet along the end grain leaving a $1/4$" tongue. Then rip the piece into $7/8$"-wide strips and crosscut the ends to $2 1/4$"-long pieces.

Pre-drill clearance holes in the wooden clips you've just made to accept a #8 × $1 1/4$" wood screw.

With a Cherry on Top

Again, trying to avoid admitting I have a curly maple addiction, I chose cherry for the top. Cut and glue the slab to the finished size given in the cutting list.

Appropriately, the Shakers used breadboard ends (traditionally called a "clamp") on their tops to hide the end grain and to help keep the top flat. The breadboard requires a tongue on each end of the top for the breadboard to fit over. I created the $5/16$"-thick × 1"-long tongue on the top using a straightedge to guide my router and a $3/4$" pattern bit.

Use a marking gauge at each edge to locate the tongue depth and align the straightedge to the mark. Set your bit to cut just behind the mark on the bottom side and just covering the mark on the top side to ensure the breadboards will fit snugly against the tabletop on the top side.

After the tongue is made, draw another line on it $1/2$" from the end, running the entire width of the top. At four equally spaced locations on the tongue, mark locations for the $2 1/2$"-wide tenons. Trim the tongue around the tenons, leaving them extending the full 1". This is where the breadboards and top will be pinned.

Supplies

Ball and Ball
ballandball.com or 800-257-3711

4 • 6" bed bolts, item #U60-076, $7.03 each

Olde Century Colors
oldecenturycolors.com

1 • Pint of Lamp Black acrylic latex paint, item #2022, $15.10

Rockler
rockler.com or 800-279-4441

1 • Pint of Sam Maloof Oil/Wax Finish item #58669, $20.99

10 • #8 × $1 1/4$" slotted screws, item #47256, $1.29 for pack of 12

Prices as of publication date.

Cut the two breadboard ends and plow the $1/2$"-deep groove the length of the ends for the tongue. Then lay out the areas that match up with the extended tongues and cut the $1/2$"-deep mortises in the bottom of the grooves.

Fit the breadboard ends to the top and clamp. At each extended tongue, drill a $1/4$" hole for the pin. Use a scrap piece on the underside to prevent "blowout." Remove the ends and elongate the holes to accommodate wood movement. Apply

After clamping the stretcher between the legs and drilling the bed bolt holes into the stretcher I simply dropped the nut into the previously cut mortises and bolted the base together.

Double-wide #20 biscuit slots in the braces work well to hold the wooden top fasteners (shown in the inset photo).

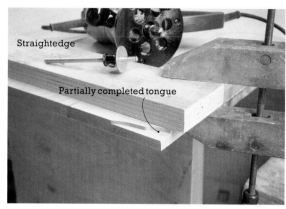

Straightedge

Partially completed tongue

With the top milled to size, mark a $5/16$"-thick × 1"-wide tongue on each end with your marking gauge. Then use a straightedge and a $3/4$" pattern bit to shape the tongue on both sides of the top.

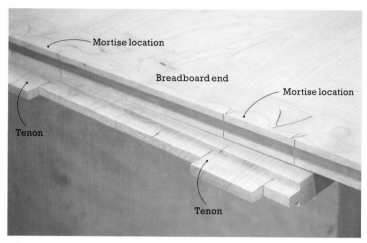

Mortise location

Breadboard end

Mortise location

Tenon

Tenon

After marking and cutting the tenons on the breadboard tongue, use the finished tenons to locate the mortises in the already-grooved breadboard ends.

glue to only the middle 4" of the tongue, reinstall the ends, then drive the pins into the holes and apply glue to only the top edge of the hole. Trim the pins and the extra length of the breadboards flush.

Finishing Touches

Sand the top with #150-grit sandpaper and rout the edges, top and bottom, with a $3/16$" roundover bit. Final sand to #180 grit and apply three to four coats of an oil/varnish blend following the product directions, then add a top coat of furniture wax.

After following the instructions in "Painting the Base" below to paint and age your base, attach the top to the base with the wooden clips and #8 × $1^1/4$" wood screws.

You and your table are now ready for years of family dinners with no concerns about sliding the ham or vegetables onto the floor because of a banquet table that's less than sturdy.

Painting the Base

A simple coat of paint on the base may suffice for many, but it looked too new and shiny for my taste, so I added an antique finish to the piece.

Begin by staining the piece and applying two coats of shellac. Sand the finish.

Next, mix Olde Century Colors Lamp Black acrylic paint with fine sawdust particles and paint the mixture onto the base. As the paint dries, wipe with a very wet rag. The wiping will remove paint and dislodge some of the sawdust pieces, leaving a "worn" surface.

Once the paint is dry, apply a coat of Maloof's Oil/Wax Finish. Simply brush it on and wipe with a clean rag. This step provides a dull sheen to the paint, adding the look of years of polish.

A simple coat of paint looks too new and shiny for a traditional Shaker piece of furniture.

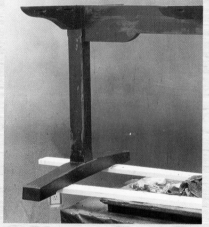

Here I've wiped the piece with a very wet cloth as the paint dried, which removed some of the paint, creating an antique finish.

Providence Writing Desk

BY MARIO RODRIGUEZ

A friend of mine recently moved into a small apartment in Providence and needed a place from which she could pay bills, do paperwork and park her computer. But the apartment is small, so the desk would be very visible. In addition to being functional, it had to look good. Needless to say, I've been looking at a lot of desks lately. And I came up with a streamlined design that has a little class; plus it fits her tastes and her space.

The design of this desk was inspired by the clean lines of Austrian Biedermeier furniture from the period 1815–1850, which preceded and influenced the popular Art Deco style. Biedermeier furniture copies the designs and elements found in both classical furniture and architecture: columns, arches, entablatures and graceful tapering legs.

The desk is compact, measuring 22" deep × 36" wide × 29¾" high, and features slender saber-shaped legs, punctuated with a small bead around each ankle and another wrapping around the desk, just below the two drawers. The generous inset dovetailed drawers are fitted with turned knobs.

The desk has a center partition that divides it in two and sits upon the drawer web (or frame). The drawers ride on the web and are guided into the interior of the desk.

In this article, I'll concentrate on the construction of the desk and only briefly mention the making and fitting of the drawers (more on drawers can be found in the February 2009 issue [#174] of *Popular Woodworking*, available to buy on popularwoodworking.com).

Selecting the Stock

I chose mahogany for its warm color, generally mild grain and wonderful working properties. It's a wood that ages well and develops a rich patina over time while surviving the inevitable nicks, dents and unintentional abuse that is the fate of furniture.

Soft maple is a good choice for the secondary wood used to make the drawer parts (sides, back and bottom), web and guides. It's strong enough for the job, machines well and is easily worked with hand tools. It also provides a nice contrast to the deep color of the mahogany. I pulled some 8/4 stock for the 1¾"-square legs, 4/4 for the skirts and top and 4/4 maple for the drawers and web frame.

After milling and squaring the leg

To maximize the length of the tenons in the rear legs, the ends are mitered.

The upper front rail is horizontal, and joins the tops of the legs with a carcase dovetail joint.

Providence Writing Desk

NO.	ITEM	DIMENSIONS (INCHES)			MATERIAL	COMMENTS
		T	W	L		
1	Top	¾	22	36	Mahogany	
4	Legs	1¾	1¾	29	Mahogany	
1	Rear apron	¾	4½	33¼	Mahogany	1¼" tenon, both ends
2	Side aprons	¾	4½	19¼	Mahogany	1¼" tenon, both ends
1	Upper front rail	¾	1⅝	33	Mahogany	1⅛" dovetail, both ends
1	Lower front rail	¾	1⅝	32¼	Mahogany	¾" tenon, both ends
1	Drawer divider	¾	3	2	Mahogany	¼" dado across back
2	Drawer fronts	¾	3	14⅜	Mahogany	
1	Beaded trim	¼	5/16	24	Mahogany	See note*
1	Beaded trim	¼	½	144	Mahogany	See note*
1	Rear upper rail	¾	2	30¾	Mahogany	Notched around legs
4	Drawer sides	⅜	3	18	Maple	
2	Drawer backs	⅜	3	14⅜	Maple	
2	Drawer bottoms	¼	18¼	14	Maple	
1	Drawer partition	¾	3	18¾	Maple	¼" tongue one end
1	Lateral rail	¾	1⅝	30	Maple	notched around legs
2	Longitudinal rails	¾	2	18⅛	Maple	¼" tongue both ends
1	Longitudinal rail	¾	4	18⅛	Maple	¼" tongue both ends
4	Drawer guides	¾	⅞	18½	Maple	

*Mill profile for beaded trim for legs and below drawers from wider piece and cut to fit lengths

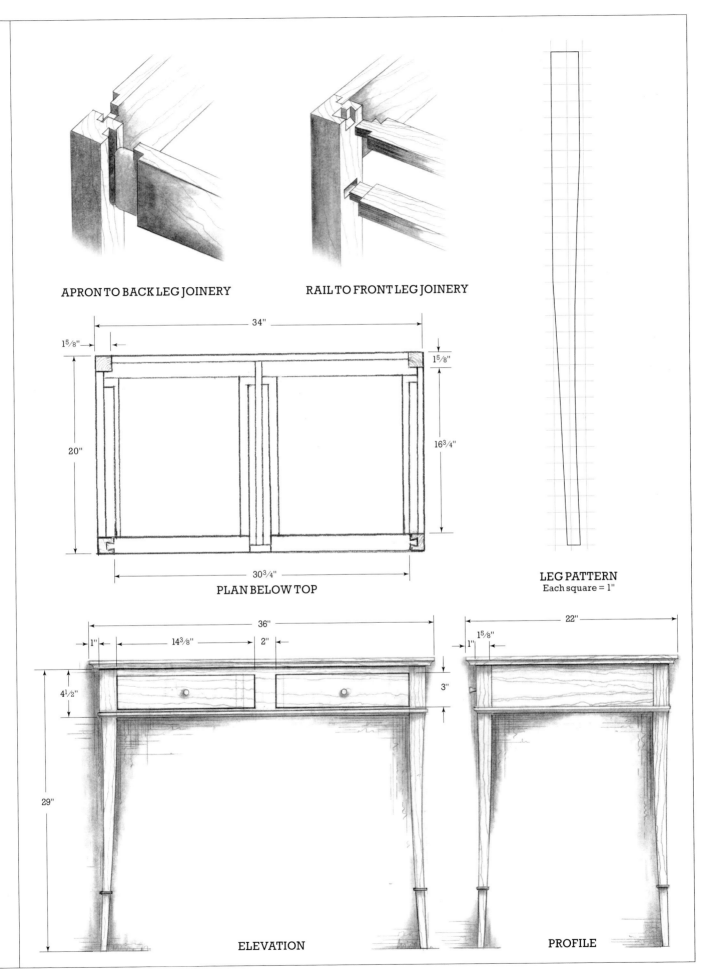

APRON TO BACK LEG JOINERY

RAIL TO FRONT LEG JOINERY

34"

1⅝"

1⅝"

20"

16¾"

30¾"

PLAN BELOW TOP

LEG PATTERN
Each square = 1"

36"

1"

14⅜"

2"

4½"

3"

29"

ELEVATION

22"

1⅝"

1"

PROFILE

stock to 1¾" and drawing the template pattern for the legs, trace the outline onto the leg blanks. Make sure to orient the outlines correctly. This is crucial to the proper placement of the mortises.

With the outlines drawn on the leg blanks, lay out the mortises. Those on the two rear legs are identical, but the right and left front legs, which are connected by the upper and lower rails that span the front of the desk, require two very different joints. The lower rail is connected by a horizontal mortise-and-tenon joint. The upper rail is attached to the leg by a carcase dovetail joint, a large single dovetail set into the top end of the leg. It maintains the critical dimensions of the desk, compensates for the smaller, weaker mortise and tenon of the lower rail, and also provides strength in case the feet of the table are forced apart. This joint should be cut by hand.

The groove for the ankle bead is cut with a ¼"-wide dado while the leg is still square. This is easy enough when using a crosscut fence fixed with a stop-block. However, the depth of the dados is not the same all around. On the back sides of the leg the dado is cut to 5⁄16" deep. On the face or front sides, it's cut to ¾". This difference produces uniform projection of the ankle bead when it's attached to the leg.

I milled the material for the apron parts and the lower front rail, which is grooved to accept the longitudinal rails, and cut them to length. Because the legs were only 1⅝" (at the top), there wasn't going to be a lot of room for the tenons. I decided on a ⅜"-thick tenon, shouldered on only one face. I was able to make them 1¼" long, but only if I mitered them.

I made all the shoulder cuts on the table saw for the best results. Then I cut the cheeks on the band saw. I always cut them just a little fat, so after a light adjustment with a shoulder plane, they fit nice and tight. Because I cut the leg mortises on a slot mortiser, they had rounded ends. Instead of squaring the mortises, I chose to round the tenons with a rasp and coarse sandpaper. The final step was to miter the ends of the tenons, so they would extend as far as possible into the mortises.

After the mortises and the dados for the beading are cut, the legs can be shaped. The curves in the legs should be carefully cut on the band saw, leaving the outline intact.

Cutting the outline on one side inadvertently removes it from the adjoining, perpendicular side, so it has to be redrawn on the uncut side, or the cutoffs (containing the outline) from the first side can be temporarily reattached with tape.

After cutting out the legs, verify the depth of the ankle dados and the location of the mortises. If everything checks out, the legs can be cleaned up and smoothed with a lineup of hand tools, starting with the spokeshave, progressing to a scraper and finishing up with #220-grit sandpaper.

When the beading is attached to the leg, it should be firmly seated into the dado and project only ⅛" (the bead's radius). For proper registration the depth of the dado should be exactly the same all around the ankle. To ensure this critical dimension, I used a small wooden gauge.

I milled the bead on the router table then cut it free, forming a delicate strip of moulding measuring ¼" by 5⁄16". This moulding is far too slender to cut with power tools, so I cut the lengths into small 2" pieces using a 16 teeth-per-inch gent's saw.

I mitered the small pieces on a horizontal belt sander fitted with a miter jig. Using this jig and sanding away material, instead of planing it, allowed me to easily "sneak up" on a clean, perfect fit. Of course, these small pieces can also be trimmed and fitted with a block plane.

When fitting the bead, work from the front or leading corner of the leg toward the back. That way the most visible miters will be tight and any small error can be hidden at the back of the ankle. I glued the pieces in with a small amount of carefully applied yellow glue, held them in place with strips of masking tape, and quickly wiped away any squeeze-out.

After testing the fit of the individual joints, I dry-fit the entire desk together and prepared for glue-up. First I glued up the legs to the side aprons. I left them clamped for a few hours, then glued and

After shaping the leg, the dados should all be the same depth. I use a simple gauge block to check the dados and adjust as necessary.

Before cutting the legs to shape, the dados for the bead are cut at the table saw. The dados on the back and inside are not as deep as on the front and outside.

The beads on the legs are too small to miter with a power saw. I cut them by hand and created the miters on the horizontal belt sander.

Fitting the leg beads begins at the outside corner. This puts the easiest joint to fit in the most visible location.

The front-to-back rails of the drawer frame are slid into the grooves, but not attached until the frame is glued inside the desk assembly.

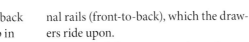

The drawer-front divider is slid between the rails and attached with screws. The partition is placed on top of the rail and behind the divider.

clamped up the side sections to the back apron and the front rails. Gluing up in stages is a lot easier than attempting the whole job at once. While it was clamped up, I checked the desk for square.

When the glue was dry, I installed the web frame parts into the desk. The web frame consists of a lateral and notched rear rail, three longitudinal rails (two side and one center), and the front rail of the desk. Both the front and rear lateral rails are grooved to accept the longitudi-

nal rails (front-to-back), which the drawers ride upon.

I inserted the tenons on the ends of the three longitudinal rails into the groove of the front rail without regard to their exact position. Then I set the rear lateral rail onto the other ends, and slid everything up into the desk. Before the glue set, I shifted and adjusted the longitudinal rails into perfect position and clamped everything up.

The small piece that divides the draw-

ers is set between the upper and lower front rails and in front of the drawer partition. In order to provide space for the drawer partition and (drawer) guides, I made this piece 3" wide, and cut the piece so the grain would run horizontally, minimizing the drawer fronts. Because the grain ran in the short direction, I cut a ¼" dado into the back to accept the tongue on the end of the drawer partition. This step stabilized and strengthened the piece.

I fit the drawer front first, then build the drawer to match the front. My process is detailed online at popularwoodworking.com/feb09.

I applied glue to the drawer partition and set its tongue into the groove on the back of the face piece, then clamped it onto the center longitudinal rail and screwed it from underneath for extra strength. Later when the glue was dry, I glued the rear upper rail to the rear apron and screwed it to the edge of the drawer partition.

With the desk assembled, I measured and cut the beaded moulding that runs around the desk, just below the drawers. I rough cut the pieces with my gent's saw, then mitered and fit the pieces using my sanding jig. When all the pieces were fitted, I attached them to the desk with glue and a small pin nailer $\frac{1}{8}$" above the bottom edge of the rails and aprons.

After the drawers were completed, I began to fit them. The fitting process was detailed in the February 2009 issue of *Popular Woodworking*. The drawer guides were rabbeted and cut 2" shy of the back apron, so they could easily be

trimmed with a regular block plane. I intentionally made them oversized to intrude into the drawer opening and prevent the drawers from sliding home.

In order to fit the drawers, I carefully planed the guides, a few light strokes at a time, so the drawers could barely squeeze in. Next, I planed a little from each guide until I achieved an attractive and even spacing on both sides. Later I would plane a small rabbet on the bottom edge of the drawer front and plane the top edge of the drawer front to create an even gap all around the drawers' openings.

I thought that wood knobs, instead of metal, would create a warmer, friendlier feeling. So I mounted a small block between centers and turned it round. Then I secured one end into my three-jawed lathe chuck, leaving one end free so I could easily shape the dome of the knob.

After reducing the diameter to $\frac{5}{8}$", I parted a shoulder about $\frac{3}{4}$" from the end.

Then I turned a slight dome on the free end and tapered the shank down to the shoulder. Using a narrow parting tool, I formed a $\frac{3}{8}$"-diameter tenon, $\frac{1}{2}$" long. The last step was to sand and finish the knobs while they were turning on the lathe.

For the top, I carefully chose three mahogany boards with straight grain and an even warm color. After arranging my boards and cutting them to rough length, I cut the edges of each board to run parallel with the straight grain. My intention was to minimize the intrusion of visible seams and to create a harmonious surface. The glued-up top successfully created the impression of a single board, and anyone viewing or inspecting it strains to locate the seams.

After fairing the seams and hand scraping the surface, I cut the top to size, allowing a 1" overhang. To relieve the edge, lighten it and create some interest, I routed a $\frac{1}{2}$" cove on the underside.

After centering the top, I drilled through the front rail and into the underside of the top. Along the front, the top was fixed, maintaining an even overhang all year long. At the back, I drilled elongated holes through the rear upper rail. These longer holes would allow the top to move, directing all the wood movement to the back of the desk.

After sanding the desk with #220-grit sandpaper, I sprayed on a coat of nitrocellulose sanding sealer. The next day, I rubbed the desk out with #0000 steel wool and sprayed on two coats of satin lacquer.

The drawer runners are rabbeted underneath and cut short to allow me to reach in and plane them with my block plane.

The knobs are turned in a three-jaw chuck. The tenon is formed, and the knobs are sanded and finished before being removed from the lathe.

The beaded trim is attached $\frac{1}{8}$" above the bottom edge of the lower rails and aprons.

White Water Shaker Table

BY CHRISTOPHER SCHWARZ

The first time I encountered this table in the White Water Shaker collection, it was locked in a storeroom with more than a dozen other pieces. To my eye, there was something unusual about it.

Was it the size? It's 25" high – a bit shorter than typical. Was it the single drawer surrounded by a solid apron? That's atypical for Shakers. Or was it something else?

I put my fingers around the front knob and slid the drawer out. And that's when the mysteries really began. The craftsmanship on the table's base is impeccable. Tight joints. Neat pins. Clean tapers. And the maker chose excellent wood – the aprons are all quartersawn walnut.

But the drawer was a different story. The drawer had one giant dovetail at each corner, and the half-blind tails at the drawer's front left a scant $1/16$" of drawer front. Further, the groove that held the drawer bottom was visible on the ends of the drawer front. That's usually a no-no.

Then I turned my attention to the tabletop. Unlike the table's base, the top was flat-sawn walnut and was thinner along its edges with an enormously wide rabbet on the underside. The top was glued and nailed to the base.

Several weeks later, I measured the table and all its details. I sat before it and stared for a long time, hoping that I would find the answers to the questions racing through my head.

Was the drawer original? Was it made by a different maker? Was the top a replacement? And what was this table used for? It's a little big for a side table. And it's too small and low for a typical worktable. But I liked it, and I resolved to build one to donate to the organization restoring the White Water village – Friends of White Water Shaker Village.

The Restoration
I decided to build this table so the wood selection and craftsmanship matched on all the components. That meant a quartersawn walnut top attached with wooden buttons and a more finely dovetailed drawer. This approach troubled me – I don't like to guess about these things. But as the table came together on my workbench, I convinced myself that I had made the right decision.

I decided to cut my drawer front from the front apron. So I ripped a $5/8$"-wide strip off the front apron. After cutting the drawer front from the apron, I glued this strip back on.

On the first day of working on the project, I glued up the slab for the top from three quartersawn walnut boards and set it aside. Then I turned my attention to the aprons, especially the front one.

After inspecting the original, I suspect the drawer opening was cut from the front apron. I decided I wanted the drawer front's grain to match the apron. So I cut the drawer front from the apron.

Here's how I did it: I started with an apron piece that was a bit wider than needed. I ripped a $5/8$" strip from the top of the front apron (this would later become the apron's top rail). Then I cut the drawer front free from the apron using a backsaw and then a plunge-cutting Japanese saw. Then I glued the $5/8$" strip back on and I had an apron with a 3" × 10" drawer hole in it.

Short & Simple Legs
The legs are $1^{11}/16$" square and taper to 1" at the floor on the two inside faces. The taper begins 1" below the apron. When selecting the stock for the legs, look for growth rings that run diagonally from corner to corner. This will ensure the legs look consistent on all four faces.

Mark out the $1/4$"-wide × $1^1/4$"-deep × 4"-long mortises on all four legs. Note that you want the aprons to be set back $1/32$" from the front face of the legs, so be sure to include that detail in your layout. Excavate the mortises.

Then you can taper the legs. I cut the tapers using a band saw and cleaned

An *azebiki nokogiri* is a Japanese saw with curved cutting blades (one for rips; the other for crosscuts). Used against a guide, you can start your cut in the middle of the apron and plunge through. This releases the drawer front from the apron.

To clean up the bottom of the drawer opening, clamp a guide to the apron and use a chisel with its flat face against the guide. Skew the tool to shear the wood and you'll find the work quite easy.

up the cuts with a jointer plane (which is safer than most table saw jigs for this operation).

(Almost) Traditional Tenons
Then turn your attention to the matching $1^1/8$"-long tenons. I sawed mine by hand. It's a challenge in wide stock such as this, but if you take your time your tenons can fit right from the saw.

I cut the face shoulders of my tenons using a Japanese flush-cutting saw and a block of wood as a guide. I simply clamped the guide on my knife line,

To cut the tenons' face shoulders you can use a scrap of wood to guide a flush-cutting saw. Just make sure the saw has no set and you've clamped the guide right on your knifed-in shoulder line.

pressed the saw against the guide and sawed a perfect shoulder.

I couldn't bear to nail and glue the top to the table's base. So I cut mortises in the four aprons that would hold buttons to allow for seasonal movement.

Then I cleaned up the legs and aprons, and prepared them for finishing.

Gluing & Pegging

I usually glue up tables in two stages. First I glue the front legs to the front apron and the back legs to the rear apron. Then I peg those tenons and legs together. Next I glue the side aprons to the front and rear assemblies, and I peg those joints.

Pegging joints can be stressful. Here's how I do it. First I make sure that my pegs and drill bit will play together nicely by making a sample joint. Sometimes pegs can be undersized, which will leave an ugly gap behind.

Then I apply painter's tape over all my joints and lay out where I want my pegs to go on the tape. To drill the hole for the peg, I use a $1/4$" brad-point bit and run the drill in reverse for a few rotations to score the perimeter of the hole. This little trick reduces tearing at the rim.

Then I drive the $1/4$" peg in with some glue and cut it flush with a flush-cut saw. The tape protects the wood from the glue and from the occasional wayward saw stroke.

The Raised-Panel Tabletop

The tabletop is a bit like a raised panel. The edges are thinned down to $1/2$" while the center field is left $3/4$" thick. This wide and shallow rabbet ($3" \times 1/4$") can be made

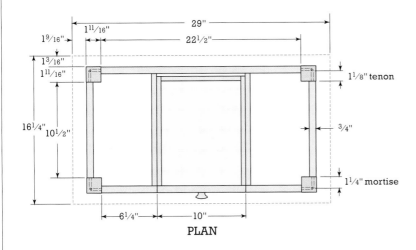

PLAN

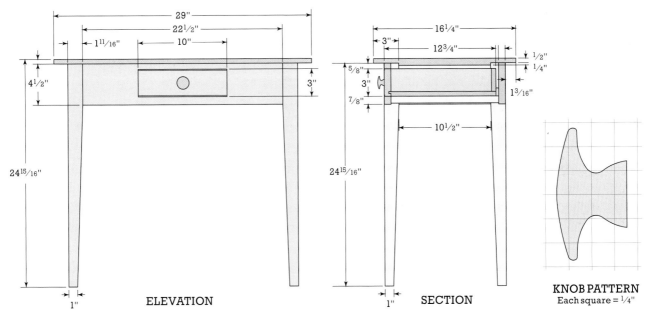

ELEVATION

SECTION

KNOB PATTERN
Each square = $1/4$"

White Water Shaker Table

NO.	ITEM	DIMENSIONS (INCHES)			MATERIAL	COMMENTS
		T	W	L		
4	Legs	$1^{11}/_{16}$	$1^{11}/_{16}$	$24^{15}/_{16}$	Walnut	
2	Long aprons	$3/4$	$4^{1}/_{2}$	$24^{3}/_{4}$	Walnut	$1^{1}/_{8}$" tenon, both ends
2	Short aprons	$3/4$	$4^{1}/_{2}$	$12^{3}/_{4}$	Walnut	$1^{1}/_{8}$" tenon, both ends
1	Top	$3/4$	$16^{1}/_{4}$	29	Walnut	
1	Drawer front	$3/4$	3	10	Walnut	Cut from front apron
2	Drawer runners	$1^{5}/_{8}$	1	$12^{5}/_{16}$	Poplar	
6	Buttons	$1/2$	1	$1^{1}/_{2}$	Poplar	
1	Knob	$3/4$	$1^{3}/_{8}$ dia.		Walnut	

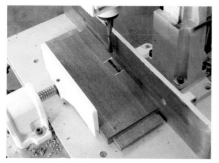

Before assembling the table's base, you should cut mortises for the buttons that will secure the tabletop to the base. I did these using a mortising machine. The mortises are $\frac{1}{4}$" wide, 2" long and $\frac{1}{2}$" deep. Poke one mortise in each end apron and two mortises in the front and back aprons.

A strip of painter's tape can protect your finished work from glue squeeze-out and from the teeth of the saw. After you cut the peg flush, remove the tape.

on the table saw or router table, but it's also quick work with hand tools. Here's how.

First cut a kerf around the center field of the panel and use a cutting gauge to define the finished $\frac{1}{2}$" thickness on all four edges. Take a rabbeting plane, tip it about 45° and run it in the kerf. Work the long edges of the tabletop first. After a few strokes, begin tilting the rabbeting plane with each stroke so it's eventually almost upright. This will create a wide "V." Work down until the "V" is $\frac{1}{4}$" deep.

Then waste away most of the rest of the wood with a fore plane or a scrub plane. Clean up the results with a block plane. After you work the long edges of the tabletop down, work the short edges in the same manner.

Attach the tabletop using shop-made wooden buttons – mine were $\frac{1}{2}$" × 1" × 1$\frac{1}{2}$". The buttons have a $\frac{1}{4}$" × $\frac{3}{4}$" lip that reaches into the mortises in the aprons. When you screw the buttons to the tabletop, the top stays in place, yet it can move with the seasons. (Note: For the buttons in the long aprons, don't bottom them out in the mortises.)

Drawers & Their Runners

The table's two drawer runners are nailed to the front and rear aprons – from the outside of the table. To make the drawer runners, take a long length of 1" × 1$\frac{5}{8}$" wood and cut a $\frac{1}{2}$" × $\frac{7}{8}$" rabbet in its long edge. Crosscut the two runners you need and fit them inside the table's base.

When you have them positioned in the right place, secure them with two cut nails (don't forget to drill pilot holes for your cut nails).

For the drawer, you can make it like the original, you can build it like I did (with three half-blind tails in the drawer's front) or build it so it suits you. I took a traditional path with my drawer. The two tails at the two back corners of the drawer are through-dovetails. The bottom is let into a $\frac{1}{4}$" × $\frac{1}{4}$" groove in the drawer sides and drawer front. The drawer bottom (like the tabletop) is also like a raised panel and slides in under the drawer's back, which is $\frac{1}{2}$" narrower than the drawer sides.

The drawer is finished up with a $\frac{3}{16}$" bead on the top and bottom edge of the front and a walnut knob. After the drawer slides smoothly, glue in a couple stops to the rear apron to make the drawer fit flush at front.

Finish & Final Thoughts

After breaking all the edges of the table with sandpaper, I added a simple and traditional finish: an oil and varnish blend. The oil gave the walnut warmth; the varnish gave it some protection. Five coats did the trick.

You can buy this finish off the shelf (Watco is one brand). Or you can make it by mixing equal parts alkyd varnish, boiled linseed oil and low-odor mineral spirits (paint thinner). Wipe on thin coats and sand away the dust nibs between coats with #320-grit sandpaper.

As a faithful reproduction, this table is a failure. I changed it too much, from the unusual original drawer to the unconventional way the top was attached on the original. But my changes were sympathetic to the time period. So though I can say this table wasn't the same as the one built in the early 19th century in southern Ohio, I can say that my version wouldn't look out of place there, either.

Remove the fence from your rabbet plane and tip the corner of the tool into the kerf as shown. After a few strokes you will reach your finished depth. Stop.

A block plane will remove most of the tool-marks from creating this large rabbet. This block plane is a rabbeting block, which allows the tool to get right into the corner.

A combination square can help line up your drawer runners and the opening for the drawer. Once everything lines up, drill your pilot holes and nail the runners in place.

The only decorative detail on the table is a small bead at the top and bottom of the drawer front. You can make this with a moulding plane or scratch stock.

Asian Coffee Table

BY CHRISTOPHER SCHWARZ

Most coffee tables are ill-equipped to handle the stresses of modern-day life. Company is coming, and your living room is strewn with books, woodworking catalogs and your spouse's catalogs. Most coffee tables offer you only a puny shelf to help you tidy up in a hurry. This coffee table does double-duty by giving you a shelf for books and two drawers that are big enough to handle all but the biggest magazines and catalogs. And oh yes, you can serve coffee on it, too.

Construction is simple but sturdy. You build the bottom case that holds the drawers out of plywood and biscuits. Then you screw the solid maple legs onto the case and cover all the plywood edges with moulding and veneer tape. Finally, you screw the top to the legs using figure-8 fasteners and build some quick drawers. And this project won't cost you a heck of a lot, either. You need about one-third of a sheet of maple plywood (birch will do just fine, too), about four board feet of 8/4 maple and about 10 board feet of 5/4 maple. You'll also need a little Baltic birch ply and a small amount of $1/4$" ply for the drawer bottoms.

Start at the Top

When you're at the lumberyard, be sure to pick through the racks of soft maple for this project. Soft maple (*Acer rubrum*) is a little cheaper than hard maple (*Acer saccharum*) and is more likely to have some curl or other figure. After you plane your maple down to 1" thickness, get ready to glue up your top. I like to cut a few biscuit slots in the mating edges of the top pieces. This doesn't add to the strength of this long-grain joint, but it sure helps keep your boards in line when gluing up your panels. Clamp up your top and set it aside for the glue to dry.

Simple & Sweet Lower Case

The case that holds the drawers goes together really fast. Cut out the parts you need according to the Schedule of Materials. Then cut the biscuit slots to attach the sides, back and divider between the top and bottom pieces. Take some care when locating the center divider to save yourself a headache when making the drawers. See the photo below for the trick to cutting biscuit slots in the middle of a panel.

Now put glue and biscuits in all the biscuit slots and clamp up the lower case. When the glue is dry, sand the case to #150 grit and turn your attention to the legs. To make attaching the legs to the case easier, go ahead and cut some clearance holes in the case's sides where the case will be joined to the back legs. This is easier to do from the outside before the legs go on.

Eight Screws & You've Got a Table

Here's how to attach the legs: Mark on the leg where the case should meet the leg. Clamp the leg into place on the lower case and then drill pilot holes and clearance holes for #8 screws (I used a bit that drills both holes simultaneously). The holes should go through the case sides and into

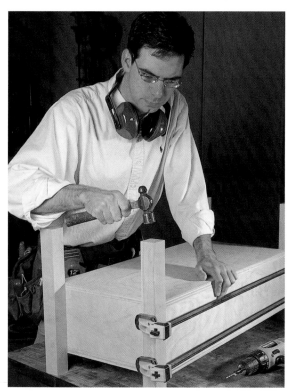

Getting the legs positioned so the table doesn't wobble is easiest to do before you screw the last leg in place (or you can spend a few hours cutting the legs with a handsaw after the table is completed; it's your choice). First clamp the fourth leg in place. Tap the top until the table sits flat. Screw the leg to the case.

Biscuiting plywood into the middle of a panel can be a layout nightmare. Or it can be a breeze. Here's the breeze way: Find the exact center of the panel and mark a line that's a hair shy of $3/8$" off from that (plywood isn't $3/4$" thick). Place the divider in place on the panel, lying flat as shown in the photo. Clamp it in place and mark the divider for a couple biscuits. Retract or remove the fence from your biscuit joiner. Cut the slots in the divider with the biscuit joiner flat on the panel. Then turn your tool around as shown in the photo and cut the slots in the panel. Use the same marks on the divider to position your tool.

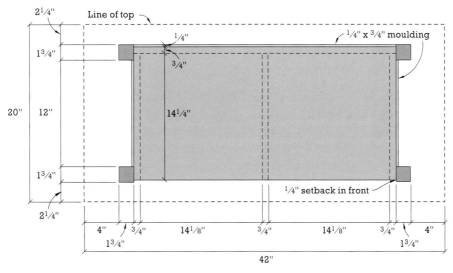

PLAN

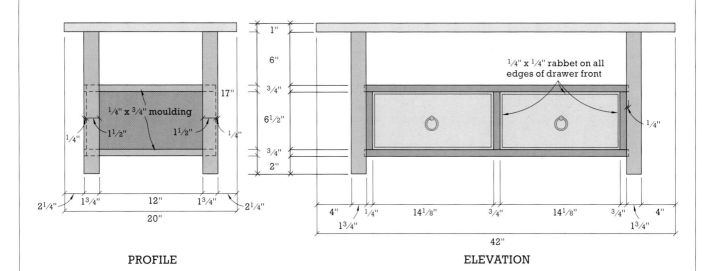

PROFILE

ELEVATION

Asian Coffee Table

NO.	ITEM	DIMENSIONS (INCHES)			MATERIAL
		T	W	L	
1	Top	1	20	42	Maple
4	Legs	$1^3/_4$	$1^3/_4$	16	Maple
2	Case top & bottom	$3/_4$	15	$30^1/_2$	Maple or birch ply
3	Sides & divider	$3/_4$	$6^1/_2$	$14^1/_4$	Maple or birch ply
1	Back	$3/_4$	$6^1/_2$	$30^1/_2$	Maple or birch ply
2	False drawer fronts	$7/_8$	$6^7/_{16}$	14	Maple
2	Drawer fronts	$1/_2$	$6^1/_4$	$13^1/_2$	Baltic birch ply
4	Drawer sides	$1/_2$	$6^1/_4$	$13^3/_8$	Baltic birch ply
2	Drawer backs	$1/_2$	$5^3/_4$	$13^1/_2$	Baltic birch ply
2	Drawer bottoms	$1/_4$	$13^1/_2$	$13^1/_8$	Maple or birch ply
	Moulding	$1/_4$	$3/_4$	10'	Maple

You want the back of the coffee table to look as interesting as the front. To mimic the divider on the front of the case, I pinned a piece of moulding in the middle of the back, too.

the legs. After the holes are drilled, screw the legs in place. Do three legs this way and clamp up the fourth leg but don't drill your holes yet.

You want to make sure that your table sits perfectly level – especially if you have hardwood floors. Place the table on a surface that you know is flat: your bench or a couple sheets of plywood. Then see if the table rocks back and forth. If your fourth leg is a little short, tap the top of the leg with a hammer until the table stops rocking. If the fourth leg is too short, turn

Supplies

Rockler
rockler.com or 800-279-4441

Desk top fasteners, item #21650, $5.49 for a pack of 8

Lee Valley
leevalley.com or 800-871-8158

2 • 40mm ring pulls, item #01A61.40, $4.50 ea.

Prices as of publication date.

the table over and tap the bottom of the fourth leg. When the table sits flat, screw the leg into place.

Trimming the Table

Now you need to cover all the exposed plywood edges on the lower case with moulding or adhesive veneer tape. I used iron-on veneer tape to cover the plywood edges around the drawers, and $1/4$" × $3/4$" maple moulding for all the other edges. Attach the moulding with glue and brads, then sand its edges flush to your case.

To make the back look a little more interesting, I added a piece of moulding to make it look like the front (see the photo above for how I did this).

Big Slab Top

Now trim your top to finished size, sand it and get ready to screw it to the table

base. Your best bet is to use figure-8 fasteners. They are quick, sturdy and let your top expand and contract with the seasons. To install them, chuck a $3/4$" Forstner bit into your drill and cut a shallow hole in the top of the leg as shown in the photo below. The depth of the hole should be the thickness of the fastener.

Screw the fasteners to the legs. Then turn your top upside down on a blanket and position the base upside down on the top. Drill pilot holes for the screws and then screw the top to the base.

Drawers

The drawers are simple plywood boxes with a solid maple drawer front screwed to the subfront. Here's how you make the plywood box. Cut your pieces to size. Then cut a $1/4$" × $1/2$"-wide rabbet on both ends of the sides. To hold the bottom in place, cut a $1/4$" × $1/4$" groove on the plywood front and sides that's $1/4$" up from the bottom edge. Nail and glue the plywood back and front between the side pieces. Slide the plywood bottom in place and nail it to the back.

Now prepare the maple drawer fronts. Cut a $1/4$" × $1/4$" rabbet on the front edges. It's a decorative detail that gives an extra shadow line around the drawers. Now screw the maple drawer fronts in place on the plywood boxes.

If you like your drawers to have a snug fit, attach a couple short pieces of veneer tape to the inside sides of the case. There's just enough space for a household iron.

Add a couple coats of clear finish and you're ready to load up your new coffee table with books, magazines and a cup of joe.

Figure-8 fasteners are perfect for this project. Be sure to cut the recess for the fastener in the position shown so the hardware will move when the top moves.

Asian Bedside Table

BY CHRISTOPHER SCHWARZ

Building cabinetry can give you a serious case of Zen Buddhism. In fact, the contradictions in woodworking are sometimes amusing – if not enlightening. Cabinets, for the most part, are more air than wood. To build a piece of furniture is mostly a process of removing wood. And to make a project look as simple and plain as this one does, it is quite a complicated process.

Now before you start worrying that this simple bedside table is too much for your woodworking skills, remember my favorite Bulgarian proverb: "If you wish to drown, do not torture yourself with shallow water."

Frames & Panels

Except for two small pieces of plywood in the sliding doors, this project is made entirely out of solid wood. To account for the seasonal expansion and contraction of the material, the table is built using a series of frame-and-panel assemblies. In a nutshell, all of the frames are connected using mortise-and-tenon joinery. The panels all rest in $3/8$"-wide × $3/8$"-deep grooves in the frames. After you have milled all the parts using the cutting list and glued up any panels you might need, I recommend you begin by building the doors.

You can see the large shoulder on the door tenon here as I'm dry-fitting the door. The large shoulder makes for a cleaner-looking tongue.

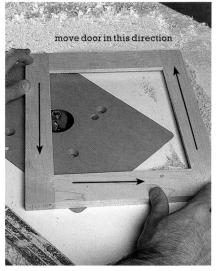

move door in this direction

You know, I really should install a starting pin in my router table for making cuts like these. If you take it slow and steady, you shouldn't have any problems. Just make sure you cut against the rotation of the cutter.

Lightweight but Solid Sliding Doors

The sliding doors on this table run in $1/4$"-wide × $1/4$"-deep grooves cut into the frame pieces. Once this table is glued up, the doors are in there for good. (You can easily make the doors removable by deepening the grooves in the top rail and increasing the width of the tongue on

Asian Bedside Table

NO.	ITEM	DIMENSIONS (INCHES)			MATERIAL	COMMENTS
		T	W	L		
Top						
2	Top stiles	$1^3/4$	$1^3/4$	30	Maple	$3/8$" × $3/8$" groove on inside edge
2	Top rails	$1^3/4$	$1^3/4$	18	Maple	1" TBE*, $3/8$" × $3/8$" groove on inside edge
1	Panel	$3/4$	$16^1/2$	$20^1/2$	Maple	In $3/8$" × $3/8$" groove; $1/2$" × $3/8$" rabbet, all sides
Base						
4	Legs	$1^3/4$	$1^3/4$	23	Maple	$3/8$" × $3/8$" groove for side & back panels
4	Rails for sides	1	$1^1/2$	14	Maple	1" TBE, $3/8$" × $3/8$" groove for side panels
3	Rails front & back	1	$1^1/2$	22	Maple	1" TBE, $3/8$" × $3/8$" groove for back panel
1	Front bottom rail	2	$1^1/2$	22	Maple	1" TBE
2	Top & bottom panels	$3/4$	$12^3/4$	$20^3/4$	Maple	$1/2$" × $3/8$" rabbet on edges; rests in $3/8$" × $3/8$" groove
2	Side panels	$3/4$	$12^5/8$	$12^5/8$	Maple	$1/2$" × $3/8$" rabbet on edges; rests in $3/8$" × $3/8$" groove
1	Back panel	$3/4$	$12^5/8$	$20^5/8$	Maple	$1/2$" × $3/8$" rabbet on edges; rests in $3/8$" × $3/8$" groove
Doors						
4	Stiles	$1/2$	$1^1/2$	$12^1/2$	Maple	
4	Rails	$1/2$	$1^3/4$	$9^1/2$	Maple	1" TBE
2	Panels	$1/4$	$8^1/4$	$9^3/4$	Ply	In $1/4$" × $3/8$" rabbet on back of door
8	Slats	$1/8$	1	$7^1/2$	Maple	Applied to panel

*TBE = tenon, both ends

the top of the doors.) To ensure the doors slide smoothly for years to come, choose straight-grained stock for the parts.

The rails and stiles of the doors are joined using mortises and tenons. The plywood panel rests in a rabbet cut in the back of the door, and the slats are merely glued onto the panel.

Begin by cutting your $\frac{1}{4}$"-thick × 1"-long tenons on the rails. As you can see in the photo on the previous page, the shoulders facing the outside edges of the door are $\frac{1}{2}$" bigger than the ones facing inside. This makes a cleaner-looking joint when you cut the tongue on the top and bottom of the door. Now cut the matching mortises in the stiles. Glue and clamp the doors.

When the glue is dry, cut a $\frac{1}{4}$"-deep × $\frac{3}{8}$"-wide rabbet on the backside of each door. Square the corners with a chisel. Finish sand the $\frac{1}{4}$" birch plywood panel and then glue it in the rabbet. When that glue is dry, glue the slats in place spaced 1" apart.

Finally, to complete the doors cut a $\frac{1}{4}$"-thick × $\frac{3}{8}$"-long tongue on the top and bottom edge of the backside of the doors.

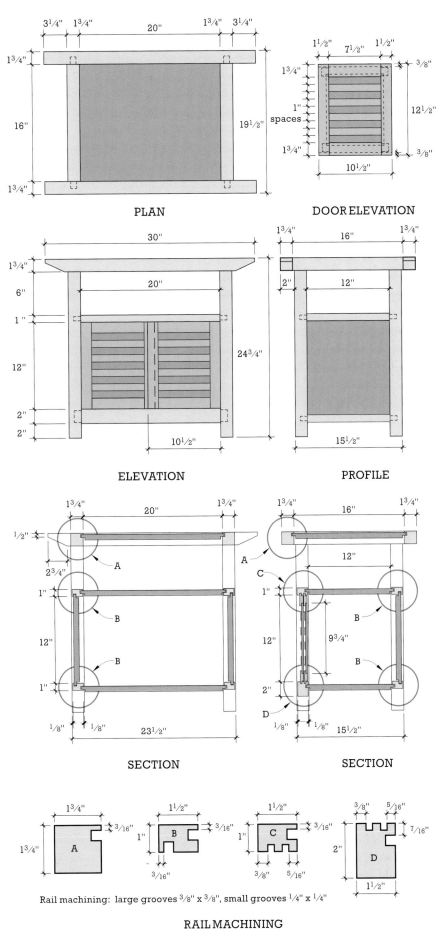

On the door slats, I cheated. I didn't feel like mortising the really thin stock into the stiles. To ensure your spacing is correct, use a couple of 1"-wide spacers to place your slats. A piece of tape on mine shimmed the spacers a bit to ensure the slats were equally spaced.

Rail machining: large grooves $\frac{3}{8}$" x $\frac{3}{8}$", small grooves $\frac{1}{4}$" x $\frac{1}{4}$"

RAIL MACHINING

The Case

Begin work on the case by cutting $\frac{1}{2}$"-thick × 1"-long tenons on all the rails with a $\frac{1}{4}$" shoulder all around. Now use your tenons to lay out the locations of the mortises on the legs. You want all of your rails to be set back $\frac{1}{8}$" from the outside edge of the legs.

The only anomaly comes when laying out the mortises for the beefy front bottom rail. Its mortises run vertically instead of horizontally.

Cut the $1\frac{1}{16}$"-deep mortises. I used a hollow-chisel mortiser equipped with a $\frac{1}{2}$" bit. As you'll see when you get into it, cutting these mortises is a bit different than in most case work. You'll clamp your work to your mortiser's fence and then move the fence in and out to cut the mortises (except when cutting the mortises for the front bottom rail, which are cut conventionally). Finally, miter the tenons so they fit in the mortises without bumping into each other.

Two Grooves for Every Rail

There are lots of grooves on the rails and in the legs. One way to cut them all is using a $\frac{3}{8}$" straight bit and a router table setup. However, I like to see what's

Again, when cutting the grooves, you want to move the router in the direction opposite the rotation of the cutterhead. In this instance, this means moving the router from left to right.

Here's where it all comes together. You can see the grooves for the panels in the rails and legs and the mitered tenons.

Quick Tips: Strategies for Ridding your Joints of Gaps

When you do a lot of mortise-and-tenon work, one of the most frustrating aspects of the joint is getting a seamless fit. Here are a few tricks to ensure fewer gaps.

1. Pay attention to the edge of the board that the mortise is in. If you sand or plane this surface before assembly, chances are you're going to change the angle of the edge, which will give you a gap when you assemble the joint. Before I cut a mortise in an edge, I run it over my jointer slowly to remove any saw marks. After the joint is glued and assembled, I go in and clean up the jointer marks with #120-grit sandpaper.

2. On highly visible joints, I'll put the tenoned piece in my vise and go to work on it with a chisel. Pare away at the shoulder area around and up to the tenon — but stay away from the edge. You only need to remove $\frac{1}{32}$" of material or so.

3. Make your mortises $\frac{1}{16}$" deeper than your tenons are long. This stops your tenons from bottoming out in the mortises and gives any excess glue a place to collect.

Supplies

Rockler
rockler.com or 800-279-4441

Desk top fasteners, item #21650, $5.49 for a pack of 8

Price as of publication date.

Micro Fence
microfence.com or 800-480-6427

going on when I cut grooves like these. So I used an aftermarket edge guide on my router. I prefer the Micro Fence for work such as this because it allows me to sneak right up on the perfect measurement with its microadjustable knob. Other edge guides are capable of the job, however.

Set your ³⁄₈" straight bit so it will make a ³⁄₈"-deep cut and set your fence so the bit is ³⁄₁₆" from the fence. Now, working from the outside edges of the rails, cut the ³⁄₈" × ³⁄₈" grooves on all the rails that hold the panels (except for the groove in the bottom front rail that holds the bottom panel). To cut that groove, set the distance between the fence and bit to ⁷⁄₁₆" and fire away. See the drawings for more details.

Now cut the grooves in the legs for the panels. Set your bit so it's ⁵⁄₁₆" from the fence and essentially connect the mortises.

Now it's time to cut the two grooves in the two front rails that the doors ride in. Chuck a ¼" straight bit in your router and cut the grooves in the top and bottom rails as shown in the drawings on page 53.

To make the panels fit in their grooves, cut a ³⁄₈"-deep × ½"-long rabbet on the underside of all the panels. You're going to have to notch the corners of each panel to fit around the legs. Cut the notches using a back saw.

Finish sand all the parts for the case and get ready for assembly. Check the fit of the doors in the grooves. A couple passes with a shoulder plane on the tongues made my doors slide smoothly. Once everything fits, glue the side assemblies up. Put glue in the mortises, but not in the grooves. You'll want to finish everything before final assembly, so set the side assemblies and the rest of the parts aside for later.

The Top: Still More Grooves

The top is made much the same as the sides. First, cut the ½"-thick × 1"-long tenons on the ends of the rails. Cut the mortises to match in the stiles. Get out your router and your fence again, chuck the ³⁄₈" straight bit in there and set the distance between the bit and the fence to ³⁄₁₆" (this will make the top recessed into the frame). Set the depth of cut to ³⁄₈" and

cut the grooves in the rails and the stiles.

Cut the detail on the ends of the stiles as shown in the drawings. I cut it using my band saw and cleaned up the bevel using a plane. Finally, cut a ³⁄₈"-deep × ½"-long rabbet on the bottom side of your panel. Finish sand all the parts and glue up the top frame.

Finish & Fit

Before finishing, apply masking tape to all the tenons and plug the mortises with packing peanuts. Apply three coats of a clear finish, such as clear shellac or lacquer, and sand between each coat. When the finish has fully cured, assemble the case. Apply glue in the mortises, slide the doors in place and clamp it up.

Check the case for square across the height and depth of the case. When the glue is dry, attach the top using desktop fasteners (sometimes commonly called "figure-8" fasteners). With a ¾" Forstner bit chucked into your hand drill, cut a recess for the fastener in the top of each leg. Screw the fasteners to the legs. Then screw the case to the underside of the top.

Whenever I finish a project such as this, I can't help but look askance at the tiny imperfections (unnoticeable to most people) that come from handwork. But then I try to remember another Zen saying from Ts'ai Ken T'An that should comfort all woodworkers: "Water which is too pure has no fish."

My large shoulder plane is probably one of the most useful tools in my shop. It trims tenons and deepens rabbets better than anything else out there. The original Record 073 (now out of production) sells used for several hundred dollars. I bought my Lie-Nielsen version for $250. Pricey? Yes, but well worth it. When you trim the tongues on the doors, make sure you have something backing up your cut or you will blow out the grain at the end.

Limbert Tabourette

BY CHRISTOPHER SCHWARZ

he curves, cutouts and captured shelf of this small table make it look like a daunting project for the beginning woodworker. But thanks to some sharp design work from our project illustrator, this tabourette actually is duck soup.

Or, should I say, "rabbet" soup.

At the core of this table is an unusual rabbet joint that joins the four legs of the table. The rabbets nest inside one another and, when assembled, look like a pinwheel when viewed from above. As a bonus, this joint allows you to make all four legs from one simple template.

But how do you clamp such a curvy form with this unusual joint? If you own a nail gun, then you already have the answer.

This noteworthy joint might be the only thing that separates my reproduction from a museum original. Using historical photographs, we went to great pains to ensure this tabourette looks exactly like the table that appeared in Charles P. Limbert Co.'s 1905 furniture catalog. If you are unfamiliar with Limbert furniture, you should know that this Grand Rapids, Michigan, company produced Arts & Crafts furniture with a European flair. Instead of straight lines and massive proportions, Limbert preferred curves. The furniture remains popular to this day. The No. 238 sold for $7 in 1905; a recent example fetched $1,600 at auction. Constructing this replica is easier than affording an original.

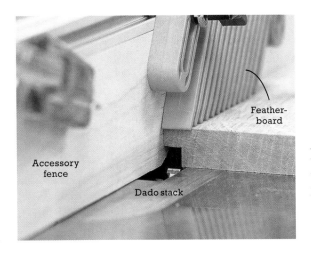

Featherboard

Accessory fence

Dado stack

An accessory fence allows you to cut rabbets on your table saw with just one pass. And a featherboard makes this joint accurate and safe.

Start With the Legs

You can build this project with just two 8'-long 1×8s, making it affordable and easy to build – even if you don't have a jointer or a planer in your shop. Limbert's company built this table in quartersawn white oak, though we've also built it in walnut and cherry for a more contemporary look.

The first order of business is, as always, to get your stock flat and true. Cut all your pieces to length and true one long edge of each board. Set aside the four boards for the legs and glue the remaining boards edge-to-edge to create the panels you will need for the top and shelf.

You're going to make the legs using a plywood template, a router and a pattern-cutting bit. But before you start cutting curves, you should first cut the ⅜" × ⅜"

rabbet on your four legs that will join the four pieces together.

This rabbet is the most critical part of the project. It needs to be precise to ensure the legs nest together seamlessly, so check your work carefully as you go. An inexpensive dial caliper will make the work easier.

I like to cut my rabbets on the table saw using a dado stack that's buried in an accessory fence. This allows me to cut my rabbets in one pass and has given me consistent results – especially when I add a featherboard to the setup, as shown in the photograph.

With your rabbets cut, fit the four pieces together to check your work. Tweak your saw's settings until everything fits. You'll be able to tune up your joints by hand later by using a traditional shoulder plane.

With the patterns taped together, attach it to a piece of plywood using a spray adhesive. This 3M product is available in the glue section of most home center stores.

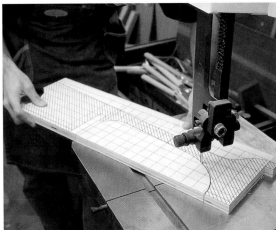

When trimming your pattern to rough size, cut as close to the line as you dare. The closer you are now, the less you'll labor your router later. But if you go over the line, you'll be in trouble.

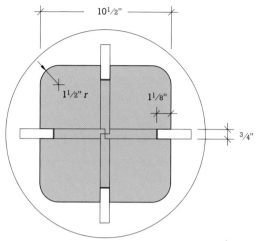

10¹/₂"

1¹/₂" r

1¹/₈"

³/₄"

PLAN – TOP REMOVED

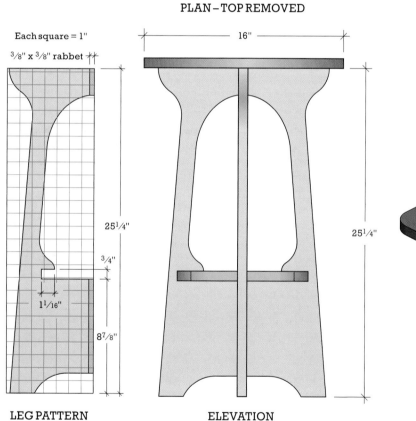

Each square = 1"

³/₈" x ³/₈" rabbet

25¹/₄"

³/₄"

1¹/₁₆"

8⁷/₈"

LEG PATTERN

16"

25¹/₄"

ELEVATION

One Template, Four Legs

With the rabbets cut, it's time to make the plywood template that will shape the legs. You can use the scaled diagrams provided, or download a full-size drawing of one from our web site (popular-woodworking.com/magazineextras; find PDF files at "Limbert Tabourette" under November 2003). The file will allow you to print out the legs on three sheets of letter-sized paper and stick them directly to your plywood with a spray adhesive. (There also is a full-size pattern of this table's shelf on our web site.) To make the template, you can use thin ¹/₄" plywood if you like, though thicker ply-

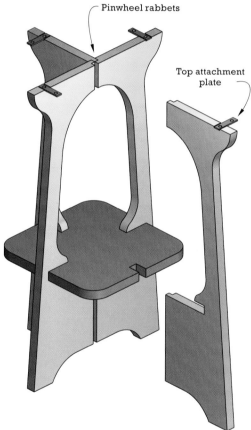

Pinwheel rabbets

Top attachment plate

EXPLODED VIEW

Limbert Tabourette

LET.	NO.	ITEM	DIMENSIONS (INCHES)			MATERIAL
			T	W	L	
A	4	legs	³/₄	8	26*	white oak
B	1	top	³/₄	16	16	white oak
C	1	shelf	³/₄	10¹/₂	10¹/₂	white oak

* Item is slightly oversized for pattern-routing

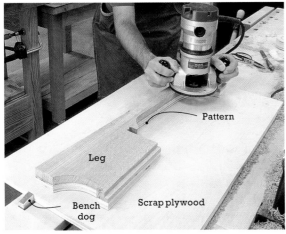

I nailed my pattern to a piece of scrap plywood and clamped that to my bench. This made routing the leg a simple operation that could be done in one pass.

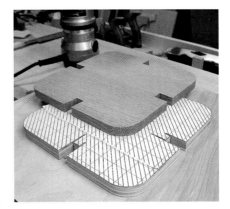

A template for the shelf can simplify things if you're making several tables. I cut the notches on each edge of the pattern with a table saw and cleaned out the interior waste with a chisel. Double-sided tape held the shelf on the pattern during routing.

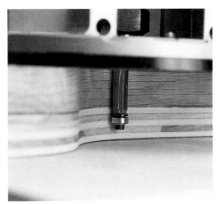

Move the router around the piece in a counterclock-wise pattern. As the grain changes direction in the piece, you might want to climb-cut a bit in places (cutting clockwise) for a cleaner cut. Just keep a firm grip on the router when you do this.

wood, such as ½" or ¾", will make your routing easier, as you'll see later on.

Using your band saw or jigsaw, cut slightly wide of the line. Leave a small nib of waste at the foot and the top of the leg that will allow you to screw this template directly to your lumber.

Clean up the curves on your template using sandpaper or files. Make the curves as smooth as possible. To ensure your curves are fair, I recommend you shape a piece of scrap with your template before you move on to the real thing. A trial run will point out rough spots or bumps that need more attention with the file.

To rout the shape of the legs, first lay the pattern on your work and line up the long, straight edge of the pattern with the rabbeted edge of the piece. Trace this shape onto your wood.

Remove the pattern and trim your leg close to this line using a jigsaw or band saw – get within 1/16" to make it easier on your router and pattern-cutting bit. Save your fall-off pieces because they can help you clamp the legs together later in the game.

There are a couple of ways to rout the legs. You can do the operation on a router table, if your table is big enough. Or you can clamp the work to your bench and use a hand-held router.

The real trick is the router bit itself. There are two kinds of pattern-cutting bits: One has the bearing at the end of the bit; the other has the bearing above the cutting flutes. I generally prefer bits with the bearing on the end, especially when

working with a hand-held router, because you can work with the pattern clamped to your workbench (if your pattern is thick enough). If this is the route you choose, clamp the pattern to your bench using a vise and bench dogs – make sure your bench dogs don't interfere with the bearing on the end of the bit. Affix the work to the pattern with screws and double-sided tape and rout it to shape.

With the shape routed, you'll immediately see that the notch that holds the shelf will need some additional work. The round router bit won't cut that area square, so square out this section with a jigsaw, band saw or even a handsaw and chisels – whatever you like. This also is the time to remove the small pieces of waste that you used to screw the work to your template.

Shape the other three legs in the same manner. Remove all the machining marks with sandpaper or hand tools (a spokeshave and smoothing plane would be appropriate). Then move on to the shelf, top and assembly.

The Other Curves
After shaping the legs, the top and shelf are pretty simple. The lower shelf

requires notches on the four sides and round corners, as shown above. You can make a template for this operation, too. Cut the notches with the same tools you used to clean up the notches in the legs.

You can round the top in a variety of ways depending on what sort of tools you have. A circle-routing jig like the one featured in our October 2003 issue ("The Magic Trammel Jig") is ideal. You also could cut it close on a band saw or jigsaw and sand it round on a disc sander.

This is the best time to finish the table's parts. Begin by sanding all the surfaces. Start with #100 grit, then move up to #180 or #220. I'm a hard-core hand-tool enthusiast so I skip the sandpaper and use a smoothing plane and a card scraper to prepare my wood for finishing. Either way is fine. Once your wood is perfect, tape off all your glue joints with blue painter's tape.

I use a tried-and-true finishing process we've developed in our shop that emulates the deep reds and browns of a fumed ammonia finish without the downsides of that dangerous chemical. We explained the entire process in detail in our June 2002 issue ("Arts & Crafts Finish," available for sale at our web site).

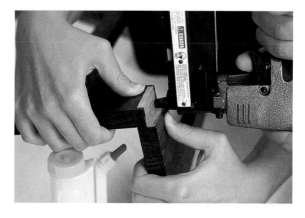

Nail one leg to the other so that the nail holes will not show when the piece is together. It's easy to do, but it's also easy to make a mistake. Use the diagram as a guide, and an extra set of hands helps immensely.

Essentially, you dye the project with a reddish half-strength water-based aniline dye. After that's dry, wipe on a coat of Valspar warm brown glaze. Then add a topcoat finish – we spray lacquer. The finish takes some time, but it's worth the effort. See the "Supplies" box below for ordering what you'll need for this finish.

Assembly

Putting the base together is easier than it looks; the trick is to do it in stages. First study the pinwheel rabbet in the diagram. Then take two of the legs and join them at a 90° angle as shown in the illustration. Here's how: Put glue in the rabbet, put the lower shelf in place and nail the two pieces together. You read that right, nail it. I've used a 23-gauge pinner and an 18-gauge nailer for this operation. Both fasteners work, but the smaller pins are less likely to split the wood.

Place the fasteners so that when you assemble the entire table the nail holes will be covered by the other rabbets. Now add

a third leg to your first assembly in the same way.

What you have left is what you see in the construction drawing: A three-legged table with a groove running down the assembly. And you have a fourth leg with its mating rabbet. Attaching this leg is a bit of a trick. I recommend either band clamps or making clamping cauls.

If you want to make clamping cauls (as shown below) you can use the fall-off pieces from band-sawing the legs to shape. These work, but they won't mate perfectly. The better way is to print out

another copy of the leg pattern and use that to saw and sand a set of cauls. To make the cauls easier to clamp to your project, tape the cauls to your clamps' heads. This allows you to assemble the project by yourself.

Using your cauls, clamp the fourth leg in place until the glue is dry, then attach the top. I used brass mending plates that have two screw holes bored in them. These simple bits of hardware allow the top to move with the seasons. To install them on the table's base, use a chisel to make a notch that's just a little bigger than the mending plate. The plate needs to pivot a bit when the top expands and contracts. (If you don't want to use mending plates, the "Supplies" box tells you where to get desk top fasteners, which function similarly.)

The notches shown in the photo are $3/32$" deep × $5/8$" wide and are $1\frac{1}{8}$" in from the outside edge of each leg. Screw each plate to the base. Once you install all four, screw the base to the top.

Now that you're done, be sure to save your templates and clamping cauls. You're ready to go into production!

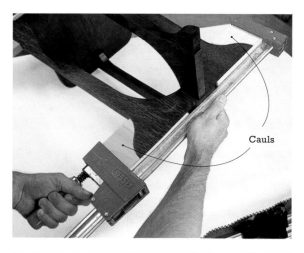

Cauls

I made clamping cauls using the patterns for the legs. Sand the edges of the cauls to avoid marring your finished edges. I also taped the cauls to my clamps, which made them easy to get in position without help.

The shallow notch at the top of each leg holds the mending plates ($1.50 for a set of four from my local home center store). Make the notch a bit wider than the plate to allow it to pivot. This allows the top to expand and contract with the seasons.

Eames-Style Coffee Table

BY CHRISTOPHER SCHWARZ

Almost any discussion of the legendary furniture designs of Charles and Ray Eames begins with plywood that has been formed into seemingly impossible shapes.

During World War II, this husband-and-wife team worked for the U.S. Navy to shape plywood under heat and pressure in ways that had not been done before. Their goal was to make lightweight splints, stretchers and even a shell for an experimental glider. But what they ended up with was the technology to create one of the most memorable pieces of 20th-century furniture: the Eames molded-plywood chair.

To complement this celebrated chair, the couple designed a coffee table similar to the one shown here. The most notable difference is that the Eames table has a top with a shallow depression in the middle that is molded from five wooden layers, also known as plies. Our top is made using solid wood and is flat.

Because few (if any) home woodworkers have the equipment to make a molded-plywood top, we decided to focus our attention on the beautifully curved and tapered legs – which usually take a back seat to the top of this famous piece of furniture.

These legs are made by gluing thin layers of wood together over a curved plywood form. When the glue dries, the legs retain the shape of the form. This process, called "cold bending," can be intimidating for woodworkers who have never tried it. However, like many things in woodworking, the barrier is only in your mind.

This simple and easy lamination is a great project for you to give this useful and strong way of bending wood a try.

A Form That Functions

Building the plywood form for the legs is simple. First, make a template from 1/4"-thick plywood or hardboard. You can use the illustration below as a guide or download a pattern from our web site (popularwoodworking.com/magazine-extras, under February 2004). Cut the curve using a band saw and smooth the edge with sandpaper.

Next, saw four pieces of 3/4"-thick plywood to the same rough shape as the template and rout them each to shape. Here's how: Simply screw the 1/4" template to your plywood. Chuck a pattern-

Even for small jobs such as making this form, using a template to rout the individual pieces ensures an accurate bend and predictable results. After the form is assembled, smooth the finished curve with sandpaper.

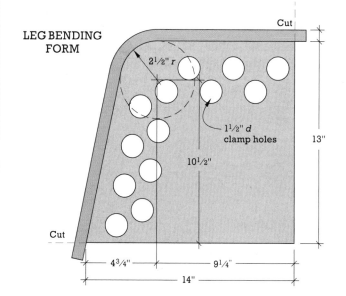

LEG BENDING FORM

Cut

$2^1/2" \, r$

$1^1/2" \, d$ clamp holes

$10^1/2"$

13"

Cut

$4^3/4"$ $9^1/4"$

14"

The band saw wastes less wood than the table saw, but it will be more work. Be sure to set up your band saw carefully for this resawing operation. Get your guides in close and set your fence for the drift of your blade.

Eames-Style Coffee Table

NO.	ITEM	DIMENSIONS (INCHES)			MATERIAL
		T	W	L	
72	Leg strips	1/16	3	33	Japanese ash
2	Braces	1	$2^3/8$	20	Poplar
1	Center block	3/4	$2^3/8$	$2^3/8$	Plywood
1	Top	3/4	34	34	Maple

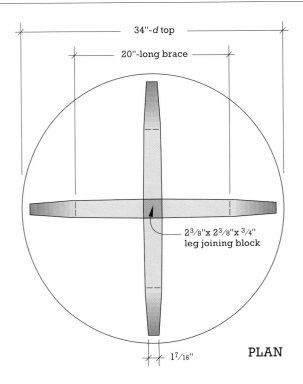

34"-*d* top

20"-long brace

$2^3/8$"x $2^3/8$"x $^3/4$"
leg joining block

$1^7/16$"

PLAN

EXPLODED VIEW

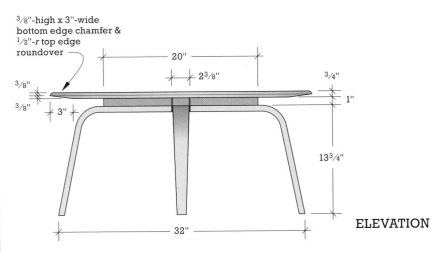

$^3/8$"-high x 3"-wide
bottom edge chamfer &
$^1/2$"-*r* top edge
roundover

$^3/8$"

$^3/8$"

3"

20"

$2^3/8$"

$^3/4$"

1"

$13^3/4$"

32"

ELEVATION

I was seduced by its arrow-straight grain – and by the fact that my lumber supplier was completely out of regular ash. I bought 18 board feet of 4/4 stock, which was enough to make six legs. You definitely want enough wood to make at least one extra leg, especially if you've never done this before.

If you are planning to resaw your plies on the table saw, it's a good idea to choose

This monster drum sander is a luxury. Luckily, there are consumer versions available from Performax and Delta. If you don't have one, chances are someone in your local woodworking club does. These are mighty handy machines.

cutting bit in your router (mine has a bearing that follows the pattern on the bottom of the bit) and trim them to finished shape.

With all four pieces of the form routed, glue and nail them into one big perfectly aligned sandwich. When the glue is dry, drill $1^1/2$"-diameter holes in the form to allow you to position your clamps' heads. I drilled 13 holes in my form in two rows: One row is centered 2" from the edge; the other is $3^1/2$" from the edge. The exact placement isn't critical – just space them evenly.

The second important part of the form is the two straight pieces of $^1/2$"-thick plywood. These pieces, which

measure 3" wide × 16" long, are clamped on top of your lamination and distribute clamp pressure evenly on your leg. They're shown in action on page 64.

Cover the working surfaces of your three form pieces with a layer of duct tape. Glue won't stick to duct tape, so this prevents you from gluing a leg to the form.

Right Wood; Right Thickness
Some woods bend better than others. Ash, hickory and oak are good choices for bending stock, whereas cherry is too brittle to easily make it around this curve without shattering.

I actually ended up using quartersawn Japanese ash, sold as "senn," for my legs.

a wood that is inexpensive, such as yellow pine. Because the plies are so thin, you're going to waste almost as much wood as you use when you cut these out on the table saw.

There is quite a good reason to use a table saw instead of a band saw for this operation: Table-sawn plies are ready to go into the form as soon as you cut them. A band-sawn ply has rough-cut surfaces that must be first sanded down in a drum sander – an expensive piece of equipment. We have a drum sander in our shop, so I opted to use the band saw.

The next step is to discover what is the thickest ply that will bend around your form. This varies from species to species. Start by cutting an $\frac{1}{8}$"-thick × 3"-wide × 33"-long ply. Try to bend it over the form using finger pressure. If the wood breaks, cut a thinner ply. If it bends, but just barely, try a slightly thinner ply. The ideal thickness for my ash was $\frac{1}{16}$", which meant I was going to have to have 12 layers of wood to create a $\frac{3}{4}$"-thick leg. In other words, to make six legs I had to saw out 72 plies (and a few extra, to account for my inevitable mistakes). Your wood species of choice might require fewer plies.

As you saw your plies, stack them in the order that they come off the saw. I marked mine on one edge so I could keep my plies together. This helps make uniform-looking legs in the end.

This simple $3 plastic paint-stirring gizmo did a better job of mixing the glue than the fancy $12 paint-stirring gizmo I own. Go figure.

Don't use too much glue, or you will just make a sliding mess when the clamps go on. A thin film on both sides is enough to do the job. Dry spots on the plies are a no-no, however.

Get Ready to Glue

Pulling off a successful bent lamination is mostly about preparation. If you have everything ready to go and have been through a dress rehearsal, you'll find it a simple and straightforward process. If you shoot from the hip, you'll end up with a messy and worthless tangle to show for your effort.

• Make sure you own or borrow enough clamps. I needed 30 bar clamps for this lamination.

• Have the right safety equipment on hand. The best glue for this job is plastic resin glue (see the "Supplies" box for ordering information). You mix it from a powder with water. If you have gloves, a face mask, goggles and long sleeves, it's easy. If you lack any of these things you're going to have irritated skin, a hacking cough and burning eyes. (Why not use yellow glue? It's flexible when it dries and will "creep" too much – the legs will lose their shape. Plastic resin glue dries harder and won't creep.)

• Pull off three 12"-long strips of duct tape and stick one end of each to your bench. You're going to wrap the lamination with these before it goes on the form. Having these on hand will save you five minutes of fumbling.

• Have your gluing equipment ready. The best way to apply the glue quickly (you can have as little as 10 minutes to do the job) is to pour it into a disposable paint tray and roll it on.

Turn off the radio, hold your calls and don't stop to chat during this part of the project. Speed and accuracy make a good lamination. This glue can set up fast. Straight parts of form (covered in duct tape) distribute clamp pressure evenly.

• Have your plies stacked exactly the way you want them and vacuum the sanding dust off them before you begin.

Once your clamps are in a row, go through a dress rehearsal without glue. Bundle your plies with a few lengths of duct tape and clamp them in the form. Start from the top of the leg and work toward the bottom. Whatever you do, don't clamp both ends and work toward the middle bend – you'll get a big ugly gap.

Take the plies off the form and get ready to mix the glue. It's time for the real thing. Plastic resin glue is messy but strong. Your best bet is to mix it up in a small bucket using a paint-stirring attachment on your cordless drill (variable speed gives you more control). To glue up one leg, I found that $1\frac{1}{2}$ cups of powder and $\frac{3}{4}$ cup of water gave me just enough for the job.

Mix the glue outside; good ventilation

is key. Slowly add the water until the glue is the consistency of heavy cream. Then stir it until all the lumps are gone. If you cannot get rid of the lumps, strain the glue through a nylon stocking or paint strainer. Then pour the glue in your paint tray.

Paint the glue on in a thin but even layer on both sides of all your interior plies. Work quickly because once the glue hits the wood, the clock is ticking. Stack your plies as soon as you've applied the glue – this slows down the glue's curing time. When all the plies are stacked, take a piece of duct tape and wrap it around the end. Tape it snugly, but by no means tourniquet-tight. Wrap the other end and the center. The duct tape minimizes the tendency of the plies to creep side-to-side.

Put the lamination on your form, put the plywood piece on top and start clamping at the top. You shouldn't break your wrist when you tighten the clamps. Snug them until the gaps close on the edges. When you get to the middle bend, push your lamination down on the form and secure it with the second piece of plywood and a clamp. It should be easier to bend than in the rehearsal – the water in the glue makes things more pliable. Then add the rest of the clamps.

Wipe the edges of the lamination with a moist rag – not too wet. Look for gaps and adjust your clamp pressure. Wait 12 hours for the glue to cure. Then repeat the whole process for the other legs.

Get Your Legs in Shape

This is the second-most fun part of the project (the big fun comes later). First you need to clean up the left edge of your lamination so you can run it through the table saw. If your jointer knives are carbide (or if they're due to be replaced), clean up one edge on your jointer. The resin glue is murder on steel knives. Otherwise, I recommend a belt sander (be wary of the dust) and then a block plane to clean up one edge.

With one edge clean, you can trim the excess junk off the top and cut the angle at the foot. This is easier than you think. After trimming the excess off the top, set your table saw's fence to $13\frac{3}{4}$". Then crosscut the foot by running the leg through the saw with the top edge flush against the fence. The photo below shows it best.

Why not just calculate the angle and cut it on your miter saw? Each leg will have a slightly different amount of "springback," which is when the leg tries to bend back to its original straight shape after coming off the bending form. Because each leg is bent at a slightly different angle, the foot angle needs to be slightly different for each, too. What a pain. Do it like the photo below shows and your legs will sit flat without geometrical equations.

Next, lay out the taper on the legs. The legs start out at $2\frac{3}{8}$" wide at the top and taper to $1\frac{7}{16}$" at the foot. To make this easier, blow up to full size the illustration below, or use it to guide you as you draw your own full-size pattern. Stick the pattern to the back side of the leg using a spray adhesive and cut the taper on the band saw.

This looks like a funky jointer operation, but the leg actually just bends around the guard, making it safe and simple. Too bad you'll have to sharpen those cutterhead knives now, but you were probably overdue.

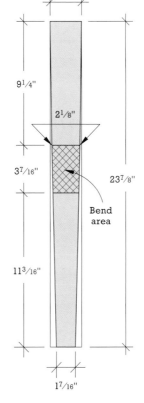

LEG TAPER PATTERN
Apply to back side of each leg

Press the top of the leg against the fence and this cut is a snap. I clamped the scrap block to the leg during the cut to prevent tear-out on the back side of the leg. Another option is to use your miter gauge and a gauge block clamped to the fence.

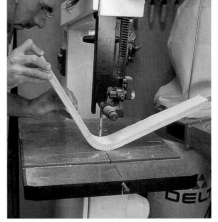

The third in our series of odd machinery operations. The band saw's blade pushes the work against the table, so it's easy to keep control of the leg as you make this bend. Still unsure? Then cut from both ends and finish the middle with a handsaw.

Supplies

Do It Best
doitbest.com or 855-828-9792

4½ lb. • DAP Weldwood plastic resin
glue, # 334178, $34.99

Price as of publication date.

"Wait a minute," you're probably saying to yourself. "How do I cut the taper on the bent part of the leg?" It's easy. Start your cut at the foot. When you get to the bend, simply tilt the leg back as shown in the photo. It looks nuts, but it's quite safe if you take it slow. After a couple of tapers, it's fun to do.

Clean up the band-sawn edges with a block plane, working from the top to the toe to reduce tearout. Sand your legs to their finished grit. Start with #100 grit and work up to #220. A word of caution: Take it easy on the inside and outside bends. It's easy to sand through a layer of your lamination, ruining your work.

Build the Braces

Sandwiched between the legs and the top are two $1" \times 2\frac{3}{8}" \times 20"$ poplar braces that are joined into an "X" shape using a half-lap joint at the center. The braces make the top sit above the legs and reveal the curve; they don't add much to the structure of the table. I laid out the half-lap joint, cut it on the band saw and cleaned it up with a chisel and shoulder plane.

Once you get the braces nesting together, screw a $\frac{3}{4}" \times 2\frac{3}{8}" \times 2\frac{3}{8}"$ block of plywood to the center of the "X." Then butt each leg against the center block and screw them to the braces.

To give the braces a clean look, trace the taper of each leg onto its matching brace. Disassemble the entire base assembly and taper the long edges of the two braces. I cut the taper on my band saw along my pencil lines and cleaned up the edges with a block plane.

A Solid Top

There are ways to make the top imitate the look of the original, but we decided a less slavish imitation was appropriate. This top has a large chamfer on the underside and a rounded top edge to give it some lightness. Once you've edge-glued

When my grandfather visited Japan he was presented with these beautiful machine-age trammels as a gift (his hosts knew he was a woodworker and engineer at heart). I use them every chance I get.

Use the handheld power planer to sculpt the chamfer on the underside. It's a free-form operation. Set your tool to take a small bite and you'll do just fine.

your boards for the top, lay out the circular shape. Then, on the underside, lay out a 28"-diameter circle. This is where you'll begin the chamfer.

Cut the top to rough shape using a band saw or jigsaw. You can then sand the sawn edge to a circular shape or rout the top round using a straight bit in your router and a circle-cutting jig.

Once your top is round, cut a round-over detail on the top edge. I used a $\frac{1}{2}"$-radius roundover bit. Then scribe a line all around the top that's exactly one-half of the thickness of the top. This is where your chamfer will end at the edge.

Before you cut the chamfer – the most enjoyable part of this table – prepare the top surface for finishing. Plane and scrape (or sand) the surface smooth.

Once that's complete, flip the top over and get out your handheld power planer. You heard me. The best way to make this chamfer is with a power tool usually used by door installers. The power planer

happens to be a champ at shaping large chamfers, too.

Work from the inside out to the edge to sculpt the chamfer and follow the grain as much as possible. Once you get within $\frac{1}{32}"$ of your two lines, move on to another section of the top. Clean up the chamfer with a block plane and a random-orbit sander.

With the top complete, it's just a simple matter of a few more screws to get the table on its feet. Screw the braces to the underside of the top. Make sure the clearance holes in the brace that crosses the grain of the top are slotted. The slots allow the top to expand and contract. Screw your legs to the braces and you're in business.

A clear finish is appropriate for this piece, as is a red dye or even an ebonized look. I sprayed on two coats of clear satin lacquer (sanding with #320-grit stearated paper between coats) and called it done.

Pleasant Hill 'Saturday' Table

BY KERRY PIERCE

ast summer I had the pleasure of visiting the Shaker Village at Pleasant Hill in Harrodsburg, Kentucky. During my stay there, the volunteer who showed me around explained that this piece is an example of something called a "Saturday table" – a table made on Saturday from bits of wood left over from the workshop's weekday labors.

I like to work in the presence of a certain amount of aesthetic risk. While I do use jigs and fixtures, I also try to preserve the need for manual skill and an educated eye. In the case of this particular piece, my original intention was to execute the legs as a high-wire act, forming their eight-tapered swelling facets completely by hand using a drawknife. However, after experimenting, I realized that – although I could produce clean surfaces with a drawknife – I might not be able to define the underlying form of each leg with enough clarity using only that one tool.

That's when I decided to build a cradle that would allow me to use the band saw to rough in the eight surfaces of each leg, surfaces I would then finish with planes, chisels and sandpaper.

First Things First

Begin by carefully prepping the lumber for the top and apron. Glue up the top, set it aside and begin working on the legs.

After milling leg blanks that finish out $1\frac{3}{4}$" on a side, turn your attention to the band saw cradle (see page 70). This doesn't have to be anything fancy. All you need is something that will hold the blank above the band saw table at a great enough height to allow it to be rotated on its centers.

Once the cradle is made, drill an $\frac{1}{8}$" hole through each of the cradle's end pieces. These holes will mark the legs' axes of rotation. On the inside surface of one of the cradle's end pieces (which I'll call the headstock end), draw a square $1\frac{3}{4}$" on a side centered on the legs' axes of rotation with its bottom line parallel to the bottom of the cradle. Then draw a second square exactly the same size and also centered on the legs' axes of rotation that is rotated 45° from the first square. Finally draw a square on the inside surface of the cradle's tailstock end that is centered on the legs' axes of rotation and parallel to the bottom of the cradle. These squares will allow you to align the leg blanks for the sawing of each leg's eight faces.

Then drill an extra hole through the end piece on the headstock end. This hole should be placed so that it is apart from the center hole and still inside each of the two squares you drew on the inside of the headstock end piece. The screw you turn into this extra hole will hold the blank in the proper alignment for each pass over the band saw.

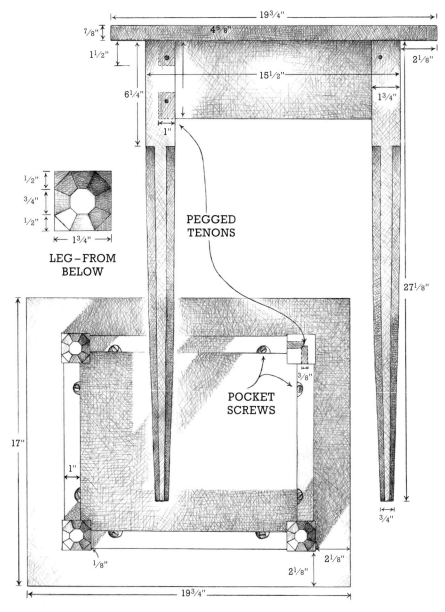

PEGGED TENONS

LEG – FROM BELOW

POCKET SCREWS

BOTTOM VIEW OF TABLE

Pleasant Hill 'Saturday' Table

NO.	ITEM	DIMENSIONS (INCHES)			MATERIAL
		T	W	L	
1	Top	$\frac{7}{8}$	17	$19\frac{3}{4}$	Walnut
4	Legs	$1\frac{3}{4}$	$1\frac{3}{4}$	$27\frac{1}{8}$	Walnut
2	Short aprons	1	$4\frac{5}{8}$	$11\frac{1}{4}$	Walnut
2	Long aprons	1	$4\frac{5}{8}$	14	Walnut

The tenons can be fine-tuned with a shoulder plane or a rabbet plane.

Paring chisels will cut the flat in each screw pocket. The rounded excavation can be made with a gouge.

Find the center of each end of each leg blank and mark it with a pencil. Then drill a shallow hole in the centers of each leg ($\frac{1}{2}$" deep, $\frac{1}{8}$" in diameter).

Turn a $1\frac{1}{4}$" #6 drywall screw through all three of the cradle end piece holes so that the points of each screw can just barely be felt on the inside surfaces of the cradle's end pieces.

Hold a leg blank in place so that its centers are positioned directly in line with the center points you marked on the inside of the cradle's end pieces. Then turn the drywall screws on each end of the cradle into the centers of each end of the leg. With the leg blank positioned so that it aligns with the single square you drew on the inside of the tailstock end of the cradle, turn the extra screw on the headstock end of the cradle into the end grain of the blank. This third screw – the set screw – will hold the blank in the correct rotational alignment for cutting the first of the leg's eight facets.

Next, you need to make a flexible pattern for marking the leg's facets. I made mine from $\frac{1}{4}$" birch plywood, but stiff cardboard would work just as well. The pattern should be as long as the full length of the leg's lower section – $20\frac{7}{8}$" – and the full width of the blank – $1\frac{3}{4}$". The taper you mark must retain enough of the leg's thickness so that after you've made the band saw cuts, you can plane away the saw marks without removing any of the leg's finished thickness. After some experimentation, I settled on a width of $1\frac{1}{4}$" at the foot of the pattern.

Lay the pattern on the blank so that its straight side aligns with one side of the leg blank and the narrow end of the pattern aligns with the foot of the blank. Then draw a line along the taper.

Place the cradle (with the leg blank attached) on the band saw and cut the first taper. Place the cradle back on the bench, back off the set screw enough so

that the leg can be rotated, then rotate the blank 90° (using the squares drawn on the cradle's headstock end piece as your guide), then turn the set screw into this new position to lock the blank in place. Use your pattern to mark the next taper, return the cradle to the band saw and saw this next facet. Repeat until the first four facets are sawn.

Then remove the blank from the cradle, plane the four sawn tapers until they're smooth, and reinstall the blank in the cradle.

Before you go any further, take a close look at the drawing of the leg and the photo of the finished table. Notice that the facets you've already cut are simply tapering extensions of the four sides of the leg's upper apron section. Notice also the next four facets – those you're about to cut – begin at shoulders which are cut in a way that connects adjacent faces of the table's square apron section.

If you haven't already done so, with your try square and a pencil, mark the bottom of the leg's four-sided apron section. Then mark a location $\frac{3}{8}$" in from each end of each of these lines on the leg blank. This will be a total of eight marks, two on each side of the apron section of the leg. Next, with a fine-toothed backsaw, cut the shoulders marking the top of the leg's other four facets. Each saw cut should connect two marks, each $\frac{3}{8}$" from the outside edges on two of the leg's adjacent faces. Be sure to cut shy of the shoulder's finished location so that you'll have material you can pare away in order to produce a finished end-grain surface.

The foot of the leg should now be a finished square measuring something in the area of 1" on a side. If it's a little more or a little less, that's fine. Make a mark $\frac{1}{4}$" from the outside of each side of the foot. Here, too, there should be eight marks.

Working by Eye

Working freehand, draw a line connecting the mark ($\frac{1}{4}$" from the outside) at the foot with the mark ($\frac{3}{8}$" from the outside) at the bottom of the apron section of the leg. The cut along that line will form the next facet of the leg. Remember that you're going to further define this line with a plane, so don't worry if it's not absolutely perfect.

Position the blank so that the top section aligns with the second square you marked on the headstock end of the cradle. Turn the set screw into the end grain of the leg blank. Working from the middle of the marked taper, saw toward both ends of the cut.

Repeat this process until the other four sides of the octagon have been roughed in.

Remove the blank from the cradle and plane this second set of facets smooth. Holding the blank in your bench vise, use a couple of your favorite planes – and a good paring chisel up under the sawn shoulders – to fine-tune the tapers on the four legs.

If possible, resist the temptation to reach for a measuring tool. This process works best if the only measurements are those made by your unassisted eye. Take a shaving or two from a facet that seems a little thin. (Remember that when you take a shaving, you actually increase the width of the facet.) Then rotate the blank in your vise. Take another shaving from

Making the Tapered Octagonal Legs

The eight sides of the tapered legs are cut on the band saw using a cradle (which can be seen in its entirety below). On one end, the headstock end, draw two squares 1³⁄₄" on a side. Each should have the same center point. One should have its bottom side parallel to the bottom of the cradle. The other is canted 45° from the first.

The leg blank is held in place by turning a screw into the center point of each end of the leg blank. The second screw on the headstock end keeps the blank in the same rotational position.

Use a pattern to draw in the first four tapers.

Cut those first four tapers by passing the cradle past the band saw blade.

After the first four tapers have been cut, fix the untapered apron section of the leg blank in your vise. Then plane away the saw marks on the taper.

After defining the shoulders of the other four facets with a backsaw, sketch in the next set of tapers freehand.

Working both ways from the middle, saw each of these facets by passing the cradle past the band saw blade.

This photo shows the leg blank in the cradle after the second set of four facets have been sawn. Notice that the top of the leg blank is aligned with the second of the two squares I drew on the inside of the headstock end piece.

The top section of each of the second set of facets can't be reached with a plane. Clean up these saw marks with a sharp paring chisel.

The two legs in front have been finished. The one immediately behind them has had the second set of facets sawn but not planed. The leg at the rear has had only the first set of facets sawn and planed, although the shoulders for the second set have been defined by a backsaw cut.

another facet if you think you need to.

In the many years I've been writing for woodworking magazines, I've had the pleasure of visiting the shops of some of this country's greatest craftsmen, and every single one routinely demonstrated the ability to find the right line – not only by measuring – but also by working with tools that were guided by the unassisted human eye. This isn't a skill they'd had since birth. This was a skill they developed over the course of many years of practice, and it is, I believe, the most important tool in their woodworking arsenal. If a line looks right, it probably is right, even if your rule shows you could make it little righter by taking off one more shaving.

Mark and cut the mortises for each of the apron tenons. (This time you should measure.)

Making the Apron
The apron sections of the Pleasant Hill original were made, I suspect, from material left over from other jobs. One apron section is 1" thick. Another is 1⅛" thick, and all four sections taper in thickness. I decided to make my aprons a consistent 1" thick.

Create the tenon thickness with a couple of passes of each apron section over a stack of dado cutters on your table saw. Then on the band saw cut away the waste to separate the two tenons on each end of each apron section.

The tenons should come off the table saw a little thicker than needed so you have some material to plane away during the final fit. Fit each tenon to each mortise.

The screw pockets on the inside of the apron should be cut before you assemble the table. These can be made on the drill press using a Forstner bit, but I chose to use chisels and gouges as the Pleasant Hill maker had done.

I started by drawing lines on the inside face of the apron sections 1" from the top edge. I then made two marks along each of these lines 1" from the shoulders. I used the intersection of these marks as the center points for 1"-diameter half circles I scribed with a compass. I used a paring chisel to cut the flat area at the top of each pocket. This flat was tilted about 70° from the outside surface

of the apron. I made the round half circle with a couple of carving gouges. You don't need to get fancy with these pockets. The ones on the original table were pretty crudely executed.

Finish each pocket by drilling a through 3/16" hole in the center of each pocket's flat spot at an angle about 90° from the surface of the pocket's flat. This will create an angle that will keep the hole from breaking out on the outside face of the apron and allow you to use 2" #6 drywall screws (coarse threaded) to hold the 7/8"-thick top in place without breaking through the top and marring the surface.

Gluing It Up
The apron sections are fairly narrow, and if your material is thoroughly dry, I think there is little chance of any cracking in response to seasonal changes in humidity, even for a table housed in a home with forced-air heat.

Nevertheless, I did take one precaution to account for any possibility of shrinkage. I undercut by 1/8" the middle edges of each tenon (the edges adjacent to the waste you removed between the tenons). This provides a little breathing room if the apron does begin to shrink across its width.

Then swab a little glue into each mortise and on each tenon and assemble the base.

Check the frame for square (when viewed from above) by measuring the diagonals of the frame. If the measurements aren't identical, apply a little pres-

Split out the pegs. Then shave them to size with a paring chisel.

sure along the longer diagonal.

Each tenon is then further secured via a round peg tapped into a drilled hole that passes through the post and through the tenon.

These pegs are best riven, splitting them out with a chisel and paring them to approximate size. They should taper from a diameter of a bit less than 1/4" on one end to a bit more than 1/4" on the other. The peg holes on the original were bored – I suspect – without measuring because there was a fair amount of variation in their placement. I bored mine in measured locations: 1/2" from the tenon shoulder and 3/4" from the top and bottom of each apron section.

Put a dab of glue on the thinner end of your peg and tap the peg – thinner end first – into the hole until it is firmly seated.

The holes on the original were bored clear through the post so that one end of the peg pokes through on the inside. I decided that mine would go in only 7/8".

Invert the top on your bench, protecting it with a towel or blanket. Then center the undercarriage and join the two parts with eight 2" #6 drywall screws. Sand and finish to suit.

Just One More Thing
If you ever get the chance to measure a piece of 18th- or early 19th-century furniture, you'll notice that – despite the solid engineering and execution you will likely see – there is far less of the obsessive perfectionism that is characteristic of some modern work and some modern woodworkers. Each side of each dovetail might slant at different angles. Each section of a table's apron might be a different thickness. Cabinet backs of even magnificent high-style work might consist of unplaned boards of random widths simply nailed into a rabbet.

In part, such imperfections are simply a reflection of the craftsman's need to get work out the door so he could get paid. But more often than not, I think, they result from the craftsman's knowledge that their clients didn't evaluate their work with a ruler and a set of dividers. They knew their clients would judge the beauty of the work with their eyes. It's not surprising, then, that often the craftsman did too.

The Lost Stickley Side Table

BY ROBERT W. LANG

Most original Gustav Stickley furniture can be easily identified by model number. This was, after all, factory-made furniture and pieces were designed to be made in multiples. When you come across an antique, you can look it up in an old catalog to identify it. However, the only known example of this small table appeared at a Sotheby's auction in late 2004.

This uncataloged piece was likely a prototype, never put into factory production. What makes it unique is the front and back splay of the legs. It's this slight angle that gives this table more character than straight-legged versions that were mass produced. It's also the likely reason this piece never got beyond the prototype stage.

This table features many of the Stickley design elements that appear in other pieces. There isn't much material in it, but there is a good deal of labor-intensive, head-scratching joinery involved. This probably made it too expensive to be marketed at a reasonable price, but that does make it a great project on which to practice and develop joinery skills.

The anonymous cabinetmaker who built this prototype lived when it was a great time to be a woodworker. Hand-tool skills had not yet been forgotten, and machinery was in use to make life in the shop easier.

As I planned how I would make this piece, I realized it made sense to do some of the work with machine methods, while on other parts it would be quicker and easier to make some joints by hand.

Using a full-size section drawing is essential; it lets me set angles and shows the exact sizes of parts without any of the risks of measuring.

First Things First

Before cutting any lumber, I made a full-size section drawing on a piece of plywood. This helped me plan the sequence of building, and the sizes of the joints. It also established a reference to the exact size and shape of the parts.

While I was building this table, I referred to this drawing rather than relying on calculations, numbers and measuring. My CAD program tells me that the angle of the legs is 3.56° and that the length of the bottom edge of the rail between the legs is 15^{17}/$_{32}$". Neither of those pieces of information is needed, and trying to build to the numbers instead of referring to the full-size drawing only slows things down and invites mistakes.

I made the legs by laminating two ^{13}/$_{16}$"-thick pieces together, then covering the edge seams with ^{1}/$_{8}$"-thick veneer that I resawed from the same boards I used for the other parts of the legs. This is the method originally used by Gustav Stickley to show quartersawn figure on all four edges of a leg. To keep the thin pieces flat, I glued and clamped all of the legs together at one time.

After trimming the edges of the veneer flush with my smoothing plane, I cut the angles at the top and bottom of each leg. I then returned to the full-size layout to locate the mortises. The mortises in each leg are in different locations, so I marked each leg's position in the table on its top. As I made other pieces, I marked which leg they joined to with a red lumber crayon.

The mortises on the back of the front legs, and the front of the back legs are parallel to the top and bottom of the legs. I put an angled block of scrap on the bed of the hollow-chisel mortiser to make these mortises.

The Best Made Plans

I planned on making the remaining mortises in the legs with the mortiser, but on the second mortise, the machine broke down. Faced with a deadline, I switched to plan B and made these mortises with my plunge router.

The through-mortises that pierce the lower front and back rails are at an angle to the face, and I'd planned to use an angled block on the bed of the mortiser to make them. Instead, I used a similar setup on the drill press. I removed most of the waste with a Forstner bit, then cleaned up the openings with chisels and rasps.

I made the straight and standard tenons on the ends of the lower rails on the table saw. I used a miter gauge to cut the tenon shoulders, and a jig that rides on the fence to cut the cheeks.

I considered making the angled cuts on the remaining tenons on the table saw, but realized each angled setup would need to be done twice: one to the right and one to the left. I decided to make a guide block that could be reversed for my handsaw, as seen in the photos at the bottom of page 75.

This was a quick and accurate method, and I was able to make all four saw cuts for each joint in sequence. This helped to keep the parts in order, and prevented making any miscuts by machine.

I dry-fitted the front and back legs with the top rails, and checked this assembly against my full-size layout. The angles matched, so I knew I could determine the length and angle of the lower stretcher directly from the full-size drawing. The critical length on this part is the distance between the shoulders of the through-tenons. The angled parts of these tenons are short, but they need to be exact. I didn't want to risk a miscut on the table saw, so I used another angled block to guide my handsaw.

The Key to a Good Fit

I did use the table saw tenoning jig to cut the wide cheeks of the through-tenons on the lower stretcher, and the band saw to cut the edge cheeks. I made all of these cuts a hair big. Through-tenons always demand some hand fitting. I used chisels, rasps and a shoulder plane to fit the tenons, checking the fit frequently as I came close to the finished size.

With the through-tenons fit, there were only two mortises remaining: those for the keys that hold the lower stretcher to the lower rails. These look difficult, but are actually the easiest joints to make in the piece. With the tenon fit in its mortise, I made a pencil mark at the intersection.

Thin veneers tend to buckle when clamped. Gluing them in a stack applies even pressure to keep them flat.

Taking the pieces back apart, I made another line slightly behind the first one. This puts the mortise just behind the intersection, and ensures that the key pulls the two lower rails tightly together. Luckily a repair part for the mortiser arrived, and I could cut these mortises with one stroke of the ½" chisel. I used a piece of scrap under the tenon to support it while the cut was made.

In most pieces with a keyed tenon, the mortise is angled slightly to allow the key to wedge in place. Because the rails

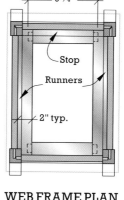

WEB FRAME PLAN

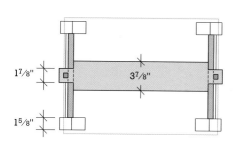

LOWER RAILS, STRETCHER & TENON KEY PLAN

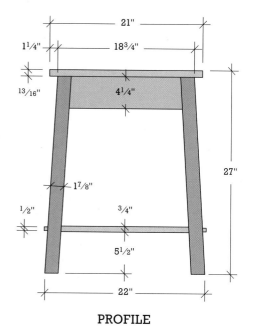

PROFILE

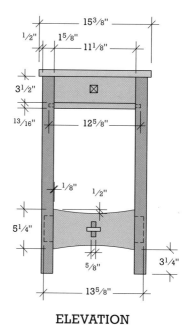

ELEVATION

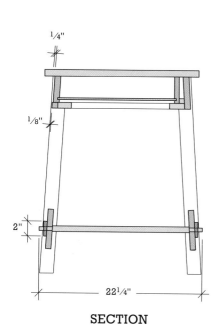

SECTION

The Lost Stickley Side Table

NO.	ITEM	DIMENSIONS (INCHES)			MATERIAL	COMMENTS
		T	W	L		
1	Top	$^{13}/_{16}$	$15^3/_8$	21	White oak	
2	Top aprons	$^{13}/_{16}$	$4^1/_4$	$17^7/_8$	White oak	$1^1/_4$" ATBE
2	Lower rails	$^7/_8$	$5^1/_4$	$13^5/_8$	White oak	$1^1/_4$" ATBE
1	Lower stretcher	$^3/_4$	$3^7/_8$	$22^1/_4$	White oak	$1^{13}/_{16}$" BSTBE
4	Legs	$1^5/_8$	$1^7/_8$	27	White oak	Angle both ends
1	Back apron	$^{13}/_{16}$	$4^1/_4$	$13^5/_8$	White oak	$1^1/_4$" TBE
1	Rail below drawer	$^{13}/_{16}$	$^{13}/_{16}$	$12^5/_8$	White oak	$^3/_4$" TBE
1	Drawer front	$^{13}/_{16}$	$3^1/_2$	$11^1/_8$	White oak	Bevel both edges to fit
2	Tenon keys	$^1/_2$	$^5/_8$	2	White oak	Taper to fit through tenons
2	Drawer sides	$^5/_8$	$3^1/_4$	$15^7/_8$	Maple	
1	Drawer back	$^5/_8$	$3^1/_4$	$11^1/_8$	Maple	
1	Drawer bottom	$^1/_4$	$10^1/_2$	$15^1/_4$	Maple	
2	Web frame stiles	$^3/_4$	2	$17^1/_4$	Poplar	Notch around legs
2	Web frame rails	$^3/_4$	2	$9^3/_4$	Poplar	$^3/_4$" TBE
2	Drawer runners	$^{11}/_{16}$	$^9/_{16}$	$15^3/_4$	Maple	Fit between legs & beside drawer
2	Drawer stops	$^{11}/_{16}$	$^9/_{16}$	6	Maple	Fit behind drawer

TBE = Tenon, both ends; BSTBE = Beveled shoulder tenon, both ends; ATBE = angled tenon, both ends

An angled block of scrap wood tilts the leg to cut an angled mortise parallel to the top of the leg.

The angled mortises on the lower rails were roughed out with a Forstner bit on the drill press. A tapered block under the workpiece makes the holes at the correct angle.

After squaring the corners of the mortise with a chisel, I use a rasp to finish smoothing the inside of the angled joint.

are tilted back and the stretcher is horizontal, the angle of the rail allows the key to wedge in a straight mortise. To make the keys, I cut a few long pieces of scrap to slightly more than the $^1/_2$" width of the mortise by $^5/_8$". I cut pieces about 6" long, and cut the taper on the band saw. I used my block plane to remove the saw marks, and bring the keys down to a snug fit.

This method let me get a good fit without worrying about the length of the keys. When I was happy with the fit, I marked $^3/_4$" above and below the protruding tenon to get the finished length of the keys.

The last parts to be made were the

narrow rail below the drawer and the web frame. The rail is thin so that it can be turned 90° to show quartersawn figure on its face. It is also beveled to be parallel with the front faces of the legs. The web frame is made from poplar, and is mortise-and-tenoned together. When I had all the joints fit, I made a dry assembly of the table. Then I took the pieces back apart so I could plane, scrape and sand all of them before gluing the entire table together.

I glued in stages, making subassemblies of front and back legs, and the top aprons. I cut some angled blocks and attached them to the top of the legs with

masking tape so that the clamps would pull straight on the angled legs.

After letting the glue dry on these, I put one of the leg assemblies flat on my bench. I put glue in the mortises, and put in the upper-back rail, the small rail below the drawer, and the lower rails, with the stretcher in place between them. I then brushed glue on the tenons, and placed the second leg assembly on top. Turning the table upright on my bench, I clamped the joints and began to worry about the drawer.

Half-blind dovetailed drawers don't bother me, but I'd never made one with the face tilted back at an angle. I decided

The quick and easy way to make the angled cuts for the through tenons is with a handsaw, guided by an angled block of wood.

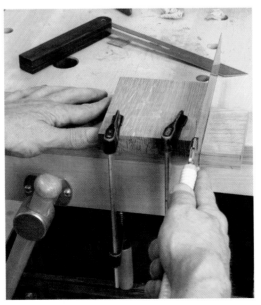

These angled shoulder cuts would be tricky to make with power tools.

After fitting the through tenon, the location of the second mortise is laid out, keeping the back of the hole just behind the face of the rail.

The mortise is cut with one plunge of the hollow-chisel mortiser. A piece of scrap below the cut supports the tenon, keeping the wood from breaking on the back side.

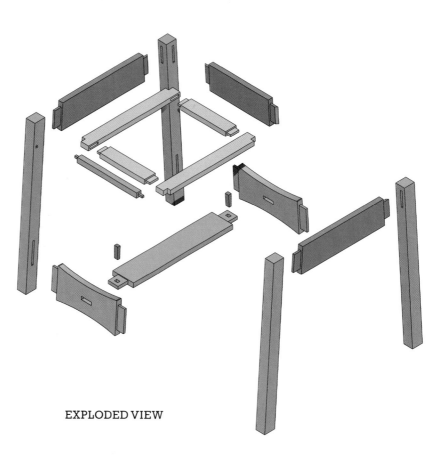

EXPLODED VIEW

As the tenon key is fit, the length above and below the through-tenon changes. I leave the key long and mark the length once I have a good fit.

After cutting the key to length, I round the edges above and below the completed joint.

The assembled web frame is notched around the legs. After fitting the drawer runners between the legs, they are screwed in place, and the drawer stop is also attached with screws to the frame.

After routing most of the waste, I use a chisel to pare the pins down the rest of the way. The router quickly establishes a consistent depth.

I laid out the tails with the same angles from horizontal that I would have if the drawer front were vertical. The knob is cut with the band saw, and shaped with a rasp.

to lay out the tails with the same angles they would have if the drawer front were vertical. This makes the top and bottom angles of the tails different in relation to the slanted drawer front which made the layout tricky, but it looked right when the joints were completed.

After cutting the tails by hand, I laid out the pins on the ends of the drawer front, and removed most of the waste with an upcut spiral bit in my trim router. This speeds things up, and gives a perfectly flat surface where the back of the tail rests on the bottom of the pin. I then used a chisel to pare down to the layout lines.

The pull was made from a cutoff piece from one of the legs. I trimmed it down to 1¼" × 1¼" by about 3" long. The pull finishes at 1⅛" but the extra length gave me something to hold on to while cutting it to shape. I laid out the shape of the pull on two adjacent faces, and cut it out on the band saw. I didn't worry about the exact size of the radius below the pyramid-shaped top; that would come from the shape of my rasp.

After cutting one face, I taped the scraps back on the block with clear packing tape and cut the adjacent side. With the rough cutting complete, I clamped the extra length in my vise, and finished shaping the pull with a rasp. The finished pull is held to the drawer front with a #8 × 1¼" screw from inside the drawer.

I wanted an authentic looking finish, but didn't want to go to the trouble of fuming it with ammonia. I used W.D. Lockwood's Dark Fumed Oak aniline dye (wdlockwood.com or 866-293-8913) diluted with alcohol. I brushed on the dye, and wiped it with a rag. I then brushed on two coats of amber shellac. After letting the shellac dry, I attached the top with figure-8 fasteners. I took off the gloss of the shellac with a Scotch-Brite pad and applied a coat of paste wax.

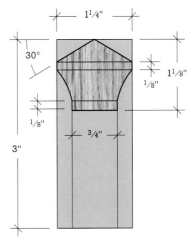

DRAWER PULL

Greene & Greene Mystery Table

BY DARRELL PEART

There is no test more demanding on a piece of furniture than that of time and service. The original example of this library table was made in the shop of brothers Peter and John Hall, who were responsible for producing the houses and furnishings designed by another set of brothers: Charles and Henry Greene. This piece has served the Hall family for nearly 100 years and is set to go a second hundred. It has passed all tests and is a tribute to the integrity of those who built it.

Most of us have furniture that we grew up with. The family places great value on this furniture, not as a national treasure, but for its history and service. As years pass, the piece is called upon to serve functions other than originally intended. Its purpose has been to serve, so it does not seem heretical to alter the piece for a new function.

This table was converted into a coffee table in the 1950s; the lower 12", which included the lower shelf, were cut off. To this day the coffee table is still faithfully serving the Hall family and graces the living room of Peter Hall's grandson. The cut-off portion has also survived.

Mystery of History

The table is solidly in the Greene & Greene style, but it is not known who designed this piece. It does not appear to be an "extra" from any known Greene & Greene project. It is possible that it was designed by one of the Halls. John Hall especially had a creative side and a highly developed sense of design.

It's a real thrill to be in the presence of furniture made by the Hall brothers, but to be given full access for hands-on examination and the chance to unlock some of the mysteries of the construction is truly heaven. As a by-product of studying the design, I gained an understanding of the designer's intentions – from the different round-overs (and their relation to one another), the arrangement of the ebony plugs and to other things impossible to explain with words.

The Halls used traditional mortise-and-tenon construction. My goal was to emulate the quality of the piece as well as the overall appearance. I kept the look of the piece as close to the original as possible while using sound alternate joinery. I made two versions of this table – one with long legs and a shelf (as in the original library table) and the other the coffee table as it exists today. If you wish to build the coffee table version, simply shorten the legs (see the illustrations) and omit the bottom shelf.

Starting in the Rough

Select material for the shelf and top core with grain match and color in mind. Rough cut the material, leaving at least 2" extra in length and at least ½" extra in width. The shelf thickness is critical to joinery later on. If you have access to a drum sander or equivalent – machine the stock and sand to exact thickness after glue-up. If not, be careful when flattening and planing the stock to minimize any tearout or snipe.

Machine to size all four legs along with all the aprons, stretchers and the

A visit to Peter Hall's grandson turned into a surprising discovery – a previously unknown piece from the Halls' shop, converted to a coffee table in the 1950s.

four small posts beside the drawer. Leave the ends and lower drawer rails ¹⁄₁₆" heavy in width to allow for cleanup when machining the cloud lifts.

Because the drawer opens from both sides there is no real back to the piece, but to keep the legs in order I arbitrarily assigned one. Bunch the legs together in their relative positions and mark them according to their position. Mark an arrow pointing to the center and mark joining lines on the facing surfaces.

Because of their strength and ease of production, I am a firm believer in floating tenons. If you have a method of your own for floating tenons or prefer traditional mortise-and-tenon joints, by all means use it. Be aware though that the lengths in the cut list do not allow for tenons – if making traditional tenons, adjust the overall length accordingly.

I used templates to locate the mortise positions (details online at popularwoodworking.com/nov07). Once the routing templates are made, set up the router with a ⅜" upcut spiral cutter and with a

¼" template guide. Rout the mortises to a depth of ⁹⁄₁₆".

Giving Yourself a Lift

Cloud lifts are a staple of the Greene & Greene style. They are easy to produce, but can be elusive if you try to shape them entirely by hand. All the cloud lifts for this project are the same size. Start by making a "master" cloud-lift template. From the drawing, lay out the cloud lifts on a piece of scrap MDF.

Band saw close to the line, then with a ½" spindle on a spindle sander (or a drill press with a ½" sanding drum) shape the inside and outside radius. Use the master template to construct templates for the end aprons and the lower drawer rails. Once the curves are machined, place blocks to register the parts and attach hold-down clamps. Remember these parts were left ¹⁄₁₆" heavy in width for this operation. Rout the parts on the router table with a flush-trim bit.

All four legs get rounded over with a ¼" radius on the edges. The three outer

Loose tenons make quick, strong joints. Using a series of templates and a guide collar locates and cuts mortises for loose-tenon joinery.

edges are rounded the entire length, the inside edge from the bottom to the dust panel. The rails, aprons and stretchers get a ⅛" roundover on exposed edges. The upper drawer rail, lower drawer rail and the drawer side posts all get a 1/16" double-stepped roundover. Use #120-grit sandpaper to achieve the second step.

The second step of the upper and lower drawer rails is trimmed to fit the drawer side posts. Use a table saw sled to shave off just the second step so the side post fits seamlessly.

Next, mill the tenon stock to a thickness of just under ⅜" and cut the tenons to length, aligning the grain with the rails. Make them about 1/16" less than the combined depth of the two corresponding mortises. Glue the tenon stock into the ends of all the aprons and rails.

How Did They Do That?
With seasonal changes in humidity the solid-wood shelf will expand and contract in the cross-grain direction. The shelf is attached to support rails in the

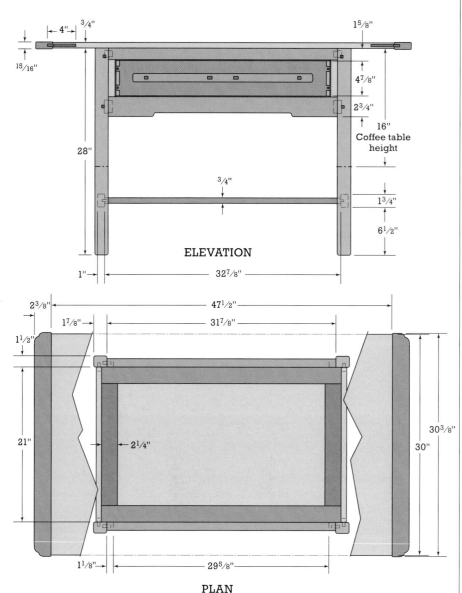

ELEVATION

PLAN

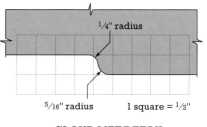

¼" radius

5/16" radius   1 square = ½"

CLOUD LIFT DETAIL

Greene & Greene Mystery Table

NO.	ITEM	DIMENSIONS (INCHES)			MATERIAL
		T	W	L	
1	Top	¾	30	47½	Mahogany
2	Breadboard ends	15/16	2⅜	30⅜	Mahogany
4	Legs	1½	1⅞	28	Mahogany
2	Side panels	¾	9¼	21	Mahogany
2	Rails above drawer	1	1 9/16	31⅞	Mahogany
2	Rails below drawer	1	2 11/16	31⅞	Mahogany
4	Posts beside drawer	1	1 1/16	31⅞	Mahogany
2	Drawer fronts	13/16	4¾	29⅝	Mahogany
2	Drawer sides	½	4¾	22⅜	Mahogany
2	Shelf rails	1	1¾	21	Mahogany
1	Shelf	¾	22½	32⅞	Mahogany
2	Dust panel rails	¾	2½	16½	Mahogany
2	Dust panel stiles	¾	2½	33⅜	Mahogany
1	Dust panel	¼	17½	29	Plywood
2	Handles	⅞	1⅛	25	Mahogany

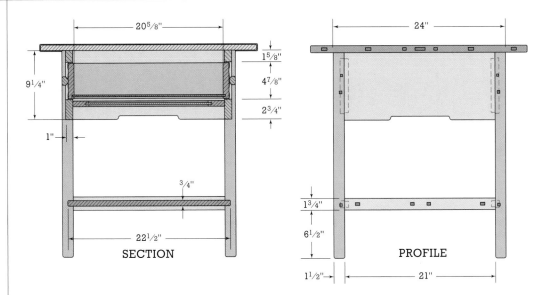

SECTION

20⅝"

9¼"

1"

22½"

1⅝"

4⅞"

2¾"

¾"

PROFILE

24"

1¾"

6½"

1½"

21"

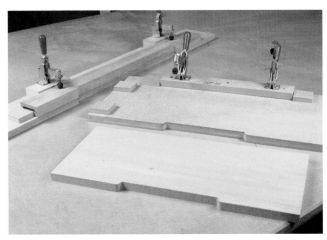

These pattern templates are used with a flush-trimming bit on the router table to generate matching shapes on the apron edges.

cross-grain direction and is captured between two legs in the same direction as well. How did the Halls deal with the obvious conflict of grain directions?

This was a question I had when I first viewed this piece. On inspection I noticed both the corner of the shelf and the leg were notched. This gave the shelf the space needed to move between the two legs – unnoticed.

But that did not solve the problem between the shelf and the rails. Looking at the ebony pegs in the shelf rails we get a clue. The outer pegs are wider than the center ones, allowing room for a slotted screw hole. The shelf can move while being held to the rails. The narrower center two holes aren't slotted.

The middle screws hold the shelf fast at the center. With the shelf fixed in the middle, it will move only half as much on either side. Each rail is essentially attached to the shelf as a breadboard end. These methods are clever and effective but the implementation is tricky.

After locating and making the square holes for the ebony plugs, rout a ¼" × ⅜"-deep spline slot centered on the back side of the shelf rail. Next drill ⅛" holes in the center two plug holes. In the outer two holes center a ⅛" × ⁷⁄₁₆" slot to allow for movement.

The exact dimensions for the shelf need to be determined. In a perfect world this is available from the drawing. The world of woodworking is not always perfect, though. The actual cuts and joinery work up to this point determine the true length of the shelf and size of its notch.

After cutting a ¹⁄₁₆"-stepped radius with a router, the remaining sharp corner is rounded over by sanding.

A portion of the stepped radius is removed at the inside corners of the drawer openings.

On paper this should be 32⅞". To find the actual length, dry assemble the leg, apron and rail pieces.

The distance between the shelf rails is the true length of the shelf. The length on paper between the notched shoulders of the shelf is 31⅞" but the actual dimension is the distance between the legs, which should be the same as the length of the drawer rails. To double-check the measurements, cut scrap wood for a test-fit of each of the dimensions.

Square the shelf then cut it to final length. Save the offcut, which should be about 2" long. Rout a ¼" × ½" spline cut centered in each end of the shelf. Rout the same spline cut in a short piece of the offcut and cut the notch as seen in the drawing using the dimension from the dry-fit for the distance between the shoulders of the notches.

Next, determine the exact location of the notch in the leg. Dry assemble the left

Two ways to deal with movement. Both the shelf and the leg are notched to help conceal seasonal wood movement.

The wider pegs at the outer ends of the shelf rail conceal slots for screws. Under the smaller pegs in the middle, the screws are in holes.

Supplies

Lee Valley
leevalley.com or 800-871-8158

Tabletop mounting clamps, item #13K01.01, $6.30 pkg. of 50

Klingspor's Woodworking Shop
woodworkingshop.com or 800-228-0000

Water-Based Dye Stain in Orange and Medium Brown, $11.95 for pint

Prices as of publication date.

and right sides of the piece. Using the off-cut from the shelf and some cross-grain spline material, mark for the notch in the leg as shown in the photo. To ensure that the location of the notch is consistent, make a spacer to register the shelf rail 6½" from the bottom of the leg. Lay out the remaining lines of the notch according to the drawing.

Use a simple routing jig to make the notch in the leg, by capturing the router base between blocks on either side and limiting the length of cut with another block. This allows the exact location of the router's cut to be visually determined.

Using a plunge router with a ½" upcut spiral bit, make a test cut with scrap material. Through trial and error determine the correct location (⅝" long rout in leg) for the rear stop block of your jig. Make another test cut to determine the exact depth of cut.

Using the actual leg, make an initial cut centered between the pencil lines and about half the final depth. Make a second cut at full depth. Move the template right and left to creep up on the pencil lines to the desired width. Test the cut with the shelf offcut piece. Once the correct cut is made, square the corners with a sharp chisel.

Next, fit the spline material in the shelf ends. Leave a ½" gap in the spline wherever a screw will pass. Glue the spline in all the way across the shelf (it will only be glued in the center 4" of the shelf rail). Be cautious of glue squeeze-out around the spline – if hardened it will obstruct a tight fit with the shelf rail.

First Subassembly

I like breaking a project down into small and manageable subassemblies. In this case I first assemble the two sets of front

Spacer

The exact location of the notch in the leg is marked from the rail using an offcut from the shelf.

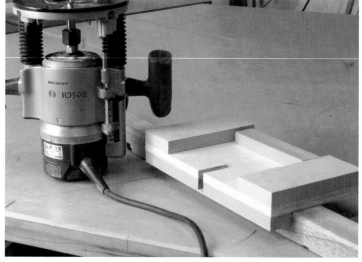

This jig traps the router base and provides a way to align the bit with the layout line.

legs to the upper and lower drawer rails and drawer side posts. Before any gluing takes place, all parts are sanded to #220 grit. I like to use a flat torsion box wrapped in butcher paper as a gluing surface to keep everything positively flat.

The floating tenons are already in the drawer rails. If the mortising went as planned, the tenons have about $1/16$" of up and down movement in the legs, allowing for precise positioning. Line up the upper drawer rail even with the top of the leg. The drawer posts will position the lower drawer rails. Take the time to dry-fit and adjust the parts if necessary. When everything is lined up, go ahead with the subassembly.

The dust panel is another case where the size on paper is not necessarily the actual size needed. The width and the length depend on the sizes of parts already made. The listed size will produce a dust panel $1/2$" too large in both directions. This lets the panel grow if necessary and allows squaring after assembly.

The dust panel's overall width should match the length of the end aprons, which on paper is 21" – defer to the actual length. To determine the length of the dust panel, dry-fit the two subassemblies to the two ends. The length between the end panels is the exact length of the dust panel. After assembling the panel in

The end cut scrap is used again to check the width of the notch in the leg.

grooves in the frame, trim it to final size and machine for biscuits that will attach it to the end apron and the lower drawer rail.

The top of the dust panel is $6^{11}/16$" down from the top of the legs. The first subassembly gives a reference for that point on both fronts of the table. Lay out and mark for the biscuits.

The Big Glue-Up

The moment of truth has arrived. It's time for the big glue-up. This is the point where my excitement level increases. Up to this point it's been a series of technical exercises. What started out as a pile of raw wood is recognizable as something approaching furniture!

The glue-up is broken down into two subassemblies. The first joins the dust panel to the two end aprons and the shelf to the shelf rail. Finish sand all parts to #220 grit before assembly. Pre-position all the clamps that will be needed and

The joinery at the shelf corners is complex, but it will remain strong and look good, making the effort worthwhile.

tape a clamp pad ($1/4$" material) where you anticipate placing a clamp.

Assemble and clamp all the parts of the table body but only apply glue to the dust panel/end apron joint and the center four-inches of the shelf spline. In the two center plug holes of the shelf rail, run a #8 × $1^1/2$" wood screw to pull the rail tight into the shelf.

Next unclamp then re-clamp, applying glue to all the areas not previously glued. Run #8 × $1^1/2$" panhead wood screws with a washer into the two outer holes of the shelf rail.

The Top: Two Kinds of Splines

The breadboard top is an exercise in dealing with seasonal wood movement. In the original, the top has contracted enough to bring the ebony spline inside the edge of the breadboard end. The Halls accounted for this when they built the piece by letting the spline float in the breadboard end. Under the top, metal corner brackets are slotted to allow for movement of the entire top.

Start by cutting the top core to overall size. Mill the breadboard ends to net size – note the breadboard ends should be $3/16$" thicker and $3/8$" longer than the top is wide. Rout a $1/4$" × $1/2$" spline groove in both ends of the core.

Reset the router depth so the bit is $1/16$" lower and rout the inside edge of the breadboard ends. This leaves the breadboard end $1/16$" proud on top and $1/8$" proud on the bottom. Next lay out and machine the seven plug holes on the exposed end of the breadboard.

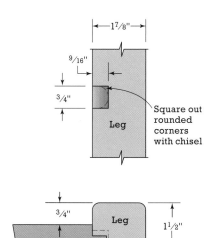

LEG AND SHELF DETAILS

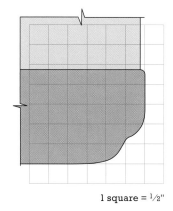

1 square = $1/2$"

BREADBOARD END DETAIL

The three center holes do not need to be drilled for screws, but the four outside holes need to have $\frac{1}{8}" \times \frac{1}{2}"$ slots machined to let the screws move with the top as it changes.

Lay out and make a full-scale MDF routing template of the breadboard ends and rout the ends to shape. All the exposed edges of the core and end get $\frac{1}{4}"$ radii, except where the breadboard end meets the top. At these points, the radii match the increased thickness of the breadboard. Be sure not to radius the end edges of the core. The spline is glued all the way across the core, but only the center four inches of the breadboard end. Leave a $\frac{1}{2}"$ gap wherever there is a screw.

We are now ready to attach the breadboard end to the core. Use one bar clamp in the center (where the glue is) to draw the two ends to the core. On either side clamp a straight edge caul that spans the core and end and keeps the assembly flat. Because the end is $\frac{1}{16}"$ proud of the top you will need $\frac{1}{16}"$-thick material to level out the surfaces under the caul. Run #10 × 2$\frac{1}{2}"$ wood screws in the outer four

plug holes on each end then remove the clamps.

The Exposed Proud Ebony Spline

There is a $\frac{5}{16}" \times 4"$ ebony spline that connects the core to the breadboard end. To make the spline, mark a pencil line on the edge of the end, $\frac{3}{4}"$ back from the joining point of the edge and core. Place a pencil mark 4" from the first line onto the core. These represent the placement of the spline. Repeat these markings on all four corners of the top.

With a spline cutter stacked to make a $\frac{5}{16}" \times \frac{1}{2}"$ deep cut, rout a slot between the lines, centered on the thickness of the core. With a chisel, square out the rounded corners left by the router in the breadboard ends. Mill stock to fit the slot. It is critical that the stock fit snugly into the slot – but not too snugly. If the stock can be removed from the slot with two fingers, it's just right!

To fit the ebony stock you will have to mimic the inside shape of the slot. I fit the slot with scrap material first then

use that as a template. To allow for movement, the spline floats in the breadboard end side. Where the spline meets the inside of the breadboard end, relieve it by about $\frac{3}{16}"$. This leaves space in the groove when the top contracts.

With the spline fit in the groove, use a white pencil or silver gel pen to trace a line about $\frac{1}{8}"$ out from the contour of the top. Waste away the outside of the line on the band saw and glue the spline in the groove, making sure not to glue the breadboard end.

The finished spline stands $\frac{1}{16}"$ proud and follows the shape of the top. To accomplish this, set a $\frac{1}{2}"$ spiral cutter with a $\frac{3}{4}"$ bearing. Level the top with the material you used for the clamping cauls and rout the spline. Replace the $\frac{3}{4}"$ bearing with a $\frac{5}{8}"$ bearing and rout again. The spline now has points at either end of the groove. Carefully trim these back with a sharp chisel until your fingers cannot snag on them. Make sure the point on the breadboard end side clears the groove. To finish the spline, ease the edges with #120-grit sandpaper and sand out any chatter on the face. Continue sanding up to #400 grit.

The Drawer

The drawer is unusual because it has no back, but instead has two fronts and opens from either face of the table. Before milling the drawer parts, verify their sizes by measuring the openings for the drawer fronts. There is a $\frac{1}{16}"$ reveal around the front, so the overall size will be $\frac{1}{8}"$ smaller than the opening.

I first cut a scrap piece of MDF to properly fit the opening. Once the correct size for the drawer is determined, mill the $\frac{13}{16}"$ drawer fronts and $\frac{1}{2}"$ drawer sides along with plenty of scrap material. (Detailed information on building the drawers is online at popularwoodworking.com/nov07).

The drawer is supported by upper and lower runners. The lower runners wrap around the bottom corners of the drawer and hold it in place side to side. The upper runners are simple rectangles in section and capture the drawer's up and down movement.

In theory, the corners in these lower runners project $\frac{1}{16}"$ proud of the lower drawer rail and drawer side posts, creat-

Assembling a complicated project goes smoothly when the process is viewed as a series of subassemblies.

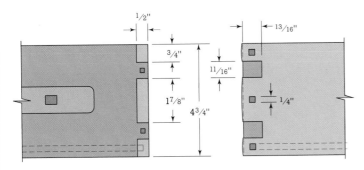

DRAWER CORNER DETAIL

The 2×4 caul keeps the face of the breadboard end parallel to the face of the top. Veneer under the caul keeps the surfaces aligned.

ing a 1/16" gap around the perimeter of the drawer. In woodworking though, theory only goes so far. In most cases a little off here and a little off there makes for adjustments later on.

Place (do not attach) the lower runners, then slide the drawer in place. Center the drawer in the openings on both sides. Make adjustments as needed to achieve an even reveal around the drawer.

If there is too much reveal at the top, shim under the lower runner. If there is too much reveal at the bottom, you may have to remove some material from the runner to compensate. When you have an even gap at top and bottom, place two thicknesses of paper between the drawer sides and lower runners.

With the runners positioned for an even gap side to side, secure the runners with #8 × 1 1/4" wood screws. Remove the paper and test the drawer for ease of action. The upper runner is actually comprised of two blocks: One 1 1/2" × 1 1/2" block that I call the anchor that is glued directly to and flush with the top of the end apron and one I call the adjuster which is screwed (no glue) to the anchor. Once the anchor is glued in place, rest the adjuster on top of the drawer side with 1/16" between.

Attaching the Top

The Halls used slotted metal corner brackets to attach the top. For convenience, I opted to use tabletop mounting clamps available from Lee Valley. These are attached to the top with screws and to the body of the table in elongated slots, allowing the top to move.

Using a biscuit joiner (or a router with a slot cutter) cut four evenly spaced slots on the inside of the upper drawer rails

and three evenly spaced slots along the upper drawer adjuster rails. The slots are 7/16" down from the top edge. With the drawer removed, place the top face down on a soft surface. Align the body of the table and use #10 × 3/4" panhead screws to secure the top.

The Finish

The finish employed by the Halls used potassium dichromate. It is a dangerous chemical to work with, so I use a dye stain that approximates the original finish.

Go over the entire piece and check for scratches or defects that need repair. Because the dye will raise the grain, the entire piece needs to be whiskered prior to dyeing. Use a damp sponge to wet the surface. When it is dry, sand lightly with #320-grit sandpaper.

For the dye, mix seven parts of General Finishes Orange dye stain with four parts of their Medium Brown dye stain, producing a beautiful brown with orange overtones. The dye stain is more user-friendly than traditional (water-soluble) aniline dyes (for ordering information, see "Supplies" box on page 82). Whereas the traditional dye would streak easily, the dye stain does not streak nearly as much.

Apply the dye in three applications with a terry cloth-covered sponge, testing first on scrap wood. Each application should be light but even. With practice the amount of dye applied can be controlled with hand pressure on the sponge.

For the top coat use General Finishes Arm-R-Seal Satin. The Arm-R-Seal offers good protection and imparts a nice

Screws hold the drawer joints together and are hidden when the ebony plugs are put in.

warm low sheen. Each coat is applied then wiped off completely when it starts to become tacky. The trick is to apply several thin coats: four to six coats for the top and three to five coats for all the rest.

If a coat tacks up too quickly and becomes difficult to remove, reapply fresh finish to loosen it up. I use compressed air to blow out finish from the nooks and crannies during the wiping-off process. Allow at least six hours and as many as 24 hours between coats, depending upon the weather conditions.

After the last coat is thoroughly dry, rub the finish out with #0000 steel wool and Mohawk brand Wool-Lube, following the instructions on the container. To complete the finish (again following the instructions on the container) apply a coat of Renaissance brand micro-crystalline wax polish. If the wax hazes up, lightly rub out with #0000 steel wool.

The table is finished! The original has been in service to the Hall family for nearly 100 years. Hopefully, 100 years from now your descendants will proudly display your table in their home.

Tapered-Leg Side Table

BY GLEN D. HUEY

Small tables are useful just about anywhere in the home. They can be easy to build, but a good design is important. To make the design more interesting, tapered legs (often part of Shaker, country and Federal furniture) are part of this design.

The taper begins below the aprons and continues on a slope until it reaches the floor. Tapering lightens the look and keeps the legs thick enough at the top to provide adequate joinery strength.

Additionally, this table's base is slightly wider than it is deep, and the top overhangs the ends more than at the front or back – the increased work surface adds to the overall design.

Where to Begin

At the home center store, pick up a piece of 1×8 red oak that's 8' long (for the top), a piece of 1×6 poplar that's 6' long and the stock for four legs – at my store I found 36"-long pieces of 2×2 poplar. Select the straightest, flattest boards you can find. And select the red oak with the best-looking grain.

At the miter saw, position a stop block to accurately cut the four legs to length. Next, cut the aprons from the 1×6, making sure to cut two each of the two different lengths. Adjust the stop block to cut the top material to length – three pieces make up the top and those three pieces need to be edge-glued.

The top has a clear finish, so it's important to examine the pieces to find the best grain match. Flip and turn the boards for the best look, one that keeps the grain flowing across the panel. Draw lines across the joints so you can easily orient the pieces into position again.

On the back face of the middle board, add three pocket-screw holes along each edge – one hole 4" off each end and center the third hole. Add a thin layer of glue to the meeting edges, orient the boards as before and install the screws while keeping

Don't limit yourself. If you understand how the parts of a table come together, there's no limit to size. Simply change the apron length, in pairs, and you can build whatever size table you like.

With the start of the taper drawn on one face, rotate the leg, mark the amount of the taper at the foot of the leg then connect the lines to show the total taper.

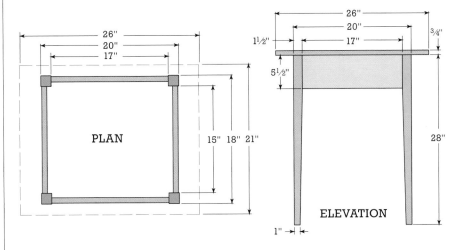

PLAN

ELEVATION

If you begin the taper cut at the foot, the task gets easier as you move up the leg. Just make sure to clamp the waste area off the side of your workbench.

the ends aligned. When done, set the panel aside while the glue dries. After 20 minutes, scrape the excess glue from the panel.

Let's Taper the Legs

The taper on tapered legs is on either two faces of the legs (as with this table), or on all four faces, which is more often seen on furniture of Federal design.

To keep things simple, work one face at a time. Move down from the top end of your legs to the width of the aprons. You could begin your taper here, but to be safe – so your taper doesn't extend up into where the apron attaches – move down another inch, then square a line across the face of the leg.

Rotate the leg 90º in either direction, slide down to the floor end of the leg and make a mark that's $\frac{1}{2}$" from the previously marked face. With the second face up, connect the end of the line with the mark set at $\frac{1}{2}$" as shown.

Securely clamp the leg to the edge of a worktable with the waste area overhanging the edge. With a sharp blade in your jigsaw, and the blade set 90° to the saw's base, carefully cut on the waste side of the line. Make the cut from the foot toward the top of the leg.

Keep the base of the saw flat to the face of the leg. The farther into the cut,

as the jigsaw base fully settles on the leg, the easier it is to keep the jigsaw square to the leg. Also, if you have a variable-speed jigsaw, turn down the speed a notch or two as you cut. This allows better control throughout the cut.

After the cut is complete, smooth the face to your layout line with a block plane. Work to maintain a 90° corner and don't worry if you plane a little bit beyond the line.

The second taper layout is made on that smoothed face. At the floor end of the leg, mark a point that's $\frac{1}{2}$" from one edge. Connect from the $\frac{1}{2}$" layout mark to the line where the taper begins on the edge nearest your $\frac{1}{2}$" mark. That line is the second cut line. Use the jigsaw to cut just off the line on the waste side, then plane the face to the line. Repeat the steps on all four legs and you have completed a set of tapered legs.

On to the Aprons

Use your pocket-screw jig to install two screw holes at both ends of each apron piece. On the long apron pieces, add two pocket-screw holes along one long-grain edge, spaced about 2" from the ends; on the short apron pieces install a single pocket-screw hole that's centered. These holes are used to secure the top, so oversize the

pocket-screw holes along the top edge of the aprons with a slightly larger diameter bit to allow for seasonal wood movement.

Gather the legs in a square with the tapers facing inward. To check the arrangement, each pair should form an inverted V-shape. If your gathering does not, rotate whichever leg is out of sorts until the V-shape is found.

On the top of the legs – the area that remains square – label each leg where the apron pieces attach. This helps keep the orientation correct throughout the construction. Before you attach the legs and aprons, sand the aprons to #120 grit.

If you attach the aprons back from the face of the legs, you'll add a nice shadow line to the design. For this, slide a scrap of $\frac{1}{8}$" hardboard under the apron before driving any screws. Clamp a leg to your worktable with the labeled face toward the apron, slide the elevated apron into position then add the screws. Next, position the second leg to the apron, clamp the leg then drive the screws. Complete two matching assemblies, then add the remaining aprons to the base.

The Top & Finish

The top's length is correct, but you'll need to trim it to width. Level the joints with a plane, sand the panel through #150 grit, including the edges, then knock off the sharp corners with sandpaper. At the same time, smooth any sharp corners on the base.

Add two coats of your favorite paint to the base and a few coats of amber shellac to the top (sanding between coats). Attach the top when it's dry. As the final touch, I added a trompe l'oeil "inlay" with the same paint as I used on the base.

Tapered-Leg Side Table

NO.	ITEM	DIMENSIONS (INCHES)			MATERIAL
		T	W	L	
4	Legs	$1\frac{1}{2}$	$1\frac{1}{2}$	28	Poplar
2	Short aprons	$\frac{3}{4}$	$5\frac{1}{2}$	15	Poplar
2	Long aprons	$\frac{3}{4}$	$5\frac{1}{2}$	17	Poplar
1	Top	$\frac{3}{4}$	21	26	Red oak

Victorian Side Table

BY MEGAN FITZPATRICK

While vacuuming a few weeks back, I was thinking about what to build when it hit me … actually, when I hit it with my vacuum. I've had a small Victorian table/bookshelf in my guest room for years, tucked away in a corner where I rarely see it. It's suffered from a broken foot for as long as I've had it. I decided the time had come to fix the problem so that I could put the table where it belongs – next to my favorite reading chair.

I headed to the home center store for select pine (4' lengths of 1×2, 1×12 and 1×8, as well as a $\frac{1}{2}$"-thick piece of pine 4" wide and 4' long – once you get out of the realm of dimensional lumber, the nominal size and actual sizes are the same). I also grabbed a 2' × 2' piece of $\frac{1}{2}$" plywood and a can of mahogany gel stain.

First, Make a Perfect Pattern

There are a great many curves in this piece – while you could use a jigsaw to cut out the sides and feet, then labori-

ously smooth and sand them with rasps, files and sandpaper, it's far easier to take the time to make one perfect pattern out of $\frac{1}{4}$" or $\frac{1}{2}$" MDF, hardboard or plywood. We prefer to use $\frac{1}{2}$" materials for patterns if we have it handy, because it gives the router bit bearing a wide surface on which to ride.

Take the time to make a good pattern and save it, so you can quickly make a

bunch of these tables should you find yourself in need of a few handmade presents for the holiday season.

I drew the entire side pattern on a piece of $\frac{1}{2}$" plywood (with the pattern's straight top edge at the factory edge of the plywood), then cut with a jigsaw about $\frac{1}{16}$" outside my lines. No matter how good the blade, the plywood will tear out a bit, so I wrapped sandpaper around a big

Trace your pattern two times on your 1×8; try to keep the grain figure centered and continuous for a good look.

dowel and used that to clean up the cuts down to the line.

Getting the pattern to look perfect may take some time – but it's worth it. Do it right (and use a sharp router bit), and you'll have almost finish-ready edges on your workpieces.

Pattern Transfer

Trace the side pattern twice on your 1×8, then cut with the jigsaw $1/8$" or so outside the curvy lines.

While you can set up for pattern routing at this point, I found it easier to first cut the two sides apart (and simultaneously make the straight cut for the top of both pieces) by using the miter saw (or you clamp a straightedge to guide the shoe of your jigsaw for a straight cut, or simply let the router make the final cut).

Now clamp the pattern in place on one side piece, and install in your router a $1/2$" straight bit with a top-mounted bearing. Adjust the depth of cut so that the blade will completely engage your workpiece, and the bearing will ride on your pattern.

For most of the work, make the cuts by moving the router from left to right, or with the direction the router bit is spinning, But as you start to move out of the grain toward the outer edge of the piece, climb-cut – that is, cut against the grain – to avoid breaking off the delicate points. Try to keep moving at a steady pace; if you leave the blade in one location for too long, you'll burn the edge of your workpiece (not a big deal – it can easily be sanded out). Also, you'll get a cleaner edge if you make one pass to remove the bulk of the waste, then ride the bearing along the pattern as you make a final light pass to cut the final shape. Do the same on the second side.

Strong Feet

You'll notice in the illustration that the feet are separate from the sides. It's important that the grain runs across the feet so that the $1 1/2$" ends don't snap off (which is exactly what happened to my antique inspiration piece). You can make a pattern and use a router to cut the feet from the end of your 1×12, but because they are simple curves, I just drew them directly on the pine, cut them with a jigsaw then sanded them.

Attach the feet to the sides with three countersunk screws – a 2" one in the middle of each foot, and 3" screws located $1 1/2$" or so to each side of center (I eyeballed it; there's no need to measure).

Shelves & Top

The shelf cleats are simply a $3/4$"-thick, $3 3/4$"-square piece, cut in half diagonally. They're secured by three $1 1/4$" countersunk screws in each. The two 20" shelf pieces are cut from the $1/2$" stock and are simply butted together at a 45° angle then secured to the cleats with three nails per end. (Don't forget to drill pilot holes.)

Cut the top cleats from the 1×2 and before screwing them down to the top of each side, round the ends with a rasp and sandpaper.

Cut the top to size, and if you like, add a decorative profile on the top edge using a $1/4$" roundover bit (or any profile you like.)

Grab your router and before you plug it in, install a $1/2$" straight bit, then adjust the depth of cut so that the blade hits your workpiece and the bearing rides on your pattern.

I stained this piece with two coats of gel stain before attaching the top, and added a top coat of wipe-on poly for protection. (Gel stain sits on top of the wood more than traditional, penetrating stain, so it cuts down a bit on the blotching inherent to pine.)

With the finish done, flip the top over, position the cleats, drill countersinks and drive $1 1/4$" screws through the cleats into the underside of the top to secure it.

Now, choose a selection of your favorite books and stock the shelf. You're ready to read.

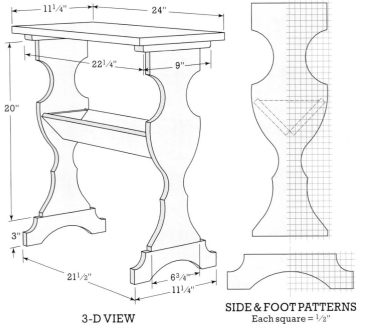

3-D VIEW

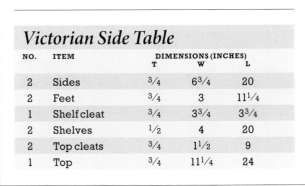

Victorian Side Table

NO.	ITEM	DIMENSIONS (INCHES)		
		T	W	L
2	Sides	$3/4$	$6 3/4$	20
2	Feet	$3/4$	3	$11 1/4$
1	Shelf cleat	$3/4$	$3 3/4$	$3 3/4$
2	Shelves	$1/2$	4	20
2	Top cleats	$3/4$	$1 1/2$	9
1	Top	$3/4$	$11 1/4$	24

SIDE & FOOT PATTERNS
Each square = $1/2$"

OTHER TABLES

Bow-Front Entry Table

BY MATTHEW TEAGUE

Learning to work with veneers and curves enables you to design and build almost anything. This bow-front entry table serves as a good introduction to both – without costing a small fortune or requiring you to attempt an overly intimidating project. Veneer introduces you to a world of beautiful grain patterns and species that are prohibitively expensive to buy in solid hardwoods. Having the confidence to add curved and veneered surfaces to your work also allows you to tackle a wide range of period, contemporary and original designs that were previously off limits.

This petite design teeters somewhere between a traditional bow-front table and a sleeker modern piece. The veneered bird's-eye maple top panel and aprons are framed and highlighted by the darker, contrasting solid cherry used for the legs and top frame. A subtle but graceful detail is that the front faces of the front legs are angled to visually extend the curve of the front apron. Like this little detail, which you may not notice at first, I think all furniture should have a few secrets to be discovered only on closer inspection. The hidden drawer on this table qualifies as well; its non-traditional placement on the side of the table is completely disguised by a drawer front that is piston-fit between the legs. Unless someone points it out, you'd never know it was there.

If you're new to veneering a curved surface or veneering altogether, this is a perfect project for expanding your skills. Thanks to a hand-pumped vacuum veneer press that costs only $60 for the complete setup, the veneering is easy,

requiring no additional veneering tools. You could, of course, skip the veneer work completely and cut the curved apron from 10/4 stock. For that matter, you could even skip building and installing the drawer. But where would be the glory in that?

Start With the Curve

I stayed away from veneer work for years; I have a small shop and didn't want to spend hundreds of dollars on a vacuum veneer press that I don't have room for. When I needed to veneer the occasional panel, I borrowed a press. But lately I've admitted that it's difficult to regularly find solid stock that looks as good as fine veneers. And even if I could, I'd get better yield by sawing it into thick veneers. So I started looking around for an affordable solution.

There are many ways to veneer curved surfaces, any of which would work for this project: You could use a vacuum veneer press to attach veneer to an MDF substrate; hammer veneer over a brick-laid curve; or clamp up laminates or bending plywood between male and female forms. But I've been curious about the hand-pumped Roarockit veneer press system, originally designed to make skateboards, since it came out (perhaps because much of my youth was well misspent on a skateboard). So I placed an order.

Whatever method you use to execute the curve, be sure to make the front apron first. Begin by drawing a full-sized version of the table base from above, as shown on page 95, but be prepared to alter the curve on the drawing if nec-

essary. Laminates have a tendency to spring back after they are bent. Once the apron comes off the form and has a chance to acclimate, check to see if there was springback. If so, adjust your full-sized drawing. Otherwise, the curve of the top may not run coplanar to the curve of the apron.

Build the Form First

The first step in making the curved apron is to make a bending form with a curve matching the drawing. My form is made of ³⁄₄" MDF, but plywood would work, too. On a scrap 5" wide × 28" long, draw out the arc as shown on page 95, bowing from 9¹⁄₂" to 12" over 24" in length. Be sure to draw the arch an additional 2" long on either end. This extra length allows you to square and tenon the ends of the front apron. Once you've band sawn the arch, refine and fair the curve with a rasp or belt sander.

Making the form takes five layers of ³⁄₄" material. Once you're happy with the fairness of the first, simply template-rout subsequent layers using a flush-trim bit on your router table. Then screw all the layers together.

It's easiest to add only one layer at a time, clamping it in place and getting the edges flush before you drive the screws. Once the form has reached full thickness, use a flexible sanding block (sandpaper glued to ¹⁄₄" plywood works well) to make sure the whole surface is smooth and fair. Laminate the apron as shown in "Hand-Pumped Veneer Press" on the next page.

While the glue sets on the curved apron, mill the rest of the table parts to rough size and then focus on the legs.

Bow a batten between finish nails driven into MDF and mark the curve. Remember to add length beyond the nails to allow for trimming and tenons.

After band sawing the curves, template-rout multiple layers of MDF and screw them together. Once the form is assembled, make sure the face is smooth and fair.

Skip the finish or wax altogether – a layer of slick packing tape is all you need to make sure glue squeeze-out won't stick to the form.

Hand-Pumped Veneer Press

Originally designed to enable non-woodworking skateboarders to build their own boards, the Roarockit veneer press works almost exactly like a vacuum veneer press, but it's small enough to stow away in a drawer when not in use – a boon for those who have small shops. Also, if you're not sure ve-neering is something you'll do often, the setup costs only $60 – a fraction of the price of a traditional vacuum press. If you find it's not your thing (you won't), you haven't risked hundreds of dollars. The price covers everything you need, including a 26" × 28" vacuum bag. Roarockit offers bags of various sizes or will make whatever size you request.

Using the Roarockit is almost identical to using a traditional vacuum press. To make the table's front apron, simply follow the steps outlined in the photos here. As you work through the process, keep a few things in mind:

Though you could veneer over an MDF or brick-laid form using this press, I glued up the apron similar to the way a skateboard is glued up. I simply laid up multiple layers of 1/16" veneers until I reached the 13/16" thickness I was after. This process is similar to laminate bending where you cut multiple layers from a single board and then glue them back together over a form. Another option would be to put the face veneer over bending plywood and a bending form. Any of these methods would work, but because the system was designed for skateboards, I borrowed as much as I could from their methods.

The only downside to simply stacking up veneer is that you have to spread a lot of glue quickly. Using thicker laminates or bending plywood – either of which would work seamlessly with the Roarockit – speeds the process. That said, I had an extra set of hands in the shop on glue-up day. With my helper and I both spreading glue we had no trouble managing the clock. Another strategy would be to use a slow-setting glue, such as urea formaldehyde or epoxy.

While skateboards are typically glued up using PVA glues (Roarockit recommends Titebond II), I took the advice of Franklin International, maker of Titebond, and used its Cold Press Glue for Veneer. In brief, regular PVAs are less brittle, which is great for, say, a skateboard that gets banged around as a matter of course. But Cold Press Glue for Veneer is a little more rigid, a bonus for furniture. It's more prone to spring-back than urea formaldehyde resin glues or epoxies (both of which are common choices for veneering and laminate bending) but it is easy to use straight out of the bottle and springback has never been an issue for me, especially on mild bends such as this one.

Once your form is made, the glue-up process is pretty straightforward; mine went off without a hitch. Just remember to make your veneers and form a little oversized so that you can square the apron's edges and ends after it comes out of the form. This project was my first experience with the Roarockit veneer press, but I suspect it's the beginning of a long and fruitful relationship.

1. Spread a thin, even layer of glue on one face of the veneer. A 4" paint roller makes this work easy.

2. After your first unglued face is on the form, stack subsequent veneer layers in place with the glued face down.

3. Spread glue on the opposing face (that way, if you miss a spot on one face the glue-up will still be OK).

4. Apply a flexible 1/8" Masonite or plywood platen over the top and tape the entire stack to the form.

5. With the glued bundle of veneer taped in place on the form, slide the assembly into the vacuum bag.

6. Netting over the top of the veneered stack provides a pathway for excess air to be sucked out of the bag once it's sealed.

7. Once the bag is sealed, a shop vacuum sucks the bulk of the air out of the bag.

8. Use the hand pump that comes with the veneer kit to remove the last of the air from the bag.

Because tenoning is the next step for the curved front apron, go ahead and cut all of the leg mortises before you taper the legs. I cut $5/16"$ mortises using my hollow-chisel mortiser and then cleaned up the walls with a chisel.

Tenon the Front Apron

Once the front apron comes off the form (you should let it sit overnight), check the curve against your initial full-sized drawing to make sure there isn't excessive springback. Using relatively thin veneers, I wound up with so little springback that I didn't need to adjust my drawing at all. (Springback may be an issue if you use thicker laminates and on more extreme curves.) If necessary, adjust the curve on your drawing and mark out the location, length and thickness of the front apron tenons on the drawing. Then mark the length, including the tenons, on the actual front apron using your drawing as a guide.

Before tenoning, square one edge of the apron at the jointer, as shown in the top left photo. Then trim the opposite edge to final width by running it through the planer.

To help square and tenon the front apron, make a quick holding jig by screwing together a few pieces of scrap and band saw them to match the curve on the inside of the apron. At the table saw, position the jig against your miter gauge with your workpiece on top of the jig. Holding the assembly firmly together (with double-sided tape if necessary), align the cut and crosscut the ends of the apron square to the edges. Because you'll use this jig again, trim the jig at the same time you trim the apron.

With the apron cut to length, mark out the location of the tenons, which you can transfer from the full-sized drawing. Attach a tall auxiliary fence to your stock table saw fence. Make a right-angle guide by attaching a guide fence flush to one edge of a $10" \times 10"$ square of MDF or plywood. Orient the right-angle guide against the tall fence so that the guide fence allows you to hold the stock upright. Then position the curved jig you just used to cut the ends to length against the right-angle guide, and the workpiece against the jig and guide. Set the height of the table saw blade to match the length

Joint one edge of the assembled front apron. Be sure one hand holds the apron flush to the fence as you square the edge to the face.

With the flattened edge facing down, guide the curved apron through the planer to square and bring the other edge parallel to the first.

Made of scrap band sawn to the shape of the inner curve and screwed in position, this simple jig positions the workpiece against a miter gauge to trim the ends square at the table saw.

With both the jig and apron cut to length, turn the jig upright against a right-angle guide and a tall fence to cut the tenon. Clamp the workpiece to the jig and the right-angle guide, align the blade to the tenon location and then cut the cheeks. The tenon shoulders are best sawn by hand.

After the tenons are fitted and the legs are ripped at an angle, the front faces of the front legs match the curve of the front apron.

Use the band saw to rip tapers on the two inside faces of the legs. Then clean up the faces using a handplane. Make sure your tapers stop at least 1/4" below the aprons.

Set your table saw blade to match the curve of the front apron and then rip the faces along their full length.

of your tenon and align the blade with the tenon location. Then make the cuts and test the fit of the tenon thickness in the leg mortises.

You could trim up the shoulders of the tenon at the table saw as well, but because it would take more extensive jigging up and there are only two of them, I used a backsaw to make the initial cuts and then fine-tuned the fit using a shoulder plane and a chisel.

Prepare the Legs

Note that the front legs of this table are cut from blanks that are wider front to back than side to side. Cutting an angle on the front of the front legs visually continues the curve of both the front apron and the tabletop. The process is simple but it lends refinement to the design. I then tapered the legs at the band saw and cleaned up the faces with a handplane.

Building the balance of the base is pretty straightforward. I veneered the

side apron and the false drawer front (both to solid maple) at the same time using the same vacuum setup I used to make the curved front apron. The side and rear apron were tenoned at the table saw, but you can use whatever method you prefer.

Assemble the Base

I've always thought that a table without a drawer, even if it has to be a small one, is a lost opportunity. Though drawers

Bow-Front Entry Table

NO.	ITEM	DIMENSIONS (INCHES)			MATERIAL	COMMENTS
		T	W	L		
1	Front apron face	1/16	3 7/16	19 5/8	Bird's-eye maple veneer	*
12	Front apron cores	1/16	3 7/16	21 3/8	Veneer*	3/4" TBE
1	Side apron core	3/4	3 7/16	6 3/4	Maple	VBS, 3/4" TBE
1	Rear apron	3/4	3 7/16	21	Maple	3/4" TBE
1	False drawer front	1/2	3 7/16	5 1/4	Maple	VBS
2	Front legs	1 5/8	2 1/8	30 1/4	Cherry	
2	Rear legs	1 5/8	1 5/8	30 1/4	Cherry	
1	Upper drawer stretcher	5/8	1 5/8	6 5/8	Maple	
1	Lower drawer stretcher	5/8	1 5/8	6 5/8	Maple	
1	Tabletop panel	3/8	8 7/8	20 7/8	MDF*	VBS, RBE
1	Tabletop frame rear	3/4	2	24	Cherry	
2	Tabletop frame sides	3/4	2	9 1/2	Cherry	
1	Tabletop frame front	3/4	4+	24	Cherry*	
2	Drawer runners	5/8	1 1/2	20 5/8	Maple	TBE
2	Drawer guides	5/8	5/8	19 1/2	Maple	
1	Drawer kicker	5/8	1 1/2	20 5/8	Maple	TBE
2	Drawer side	1/2	2 3/16	20 1/2	Maple	
1	Drawer back	1/2	2 3/16	5 1/4	Maple	
1	Drawer front	1/2	2 3/16	5 1/4	Maple	
1	Drawer bottom	3/8	4 5/8	19 7/8	Cherry	

*Cut oversize to match layout, trim to final dimensions; TBE = Tenon, both ends; VBS = Veneer, both sides; RBE = Rabbet bottom edge to fit groove in frame

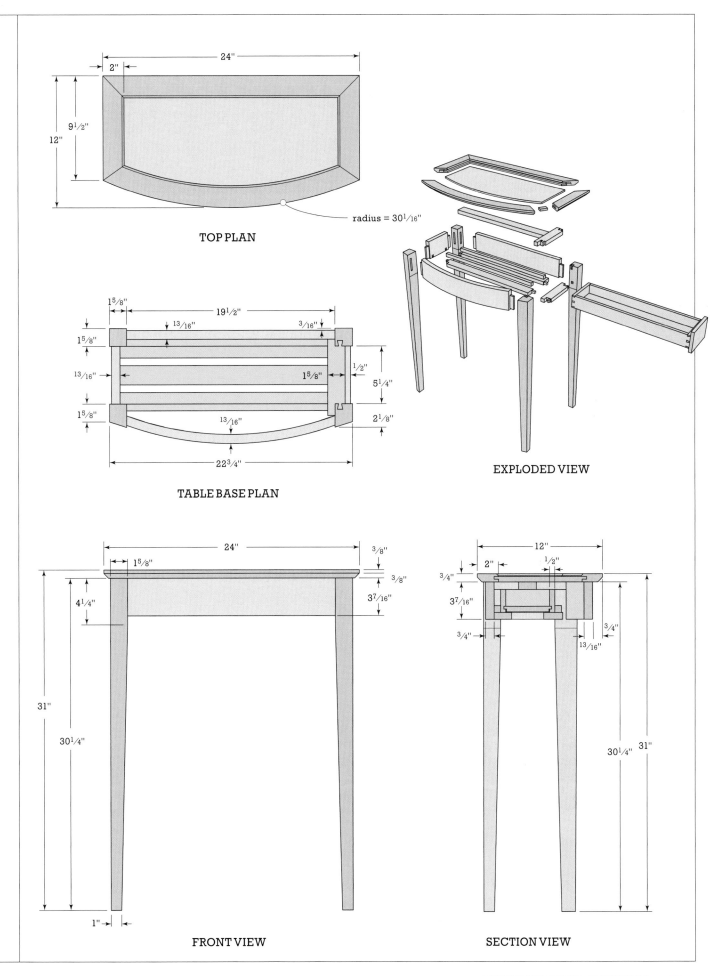

TOP PLAN

radius = $30\frac{1}{16}$"

TABLE BASE PLAN

EXPLODED VIEW

FRONT VIEW

SECTION VIEW

are traditionally placed at the front of a table, a drawer on the front of this table would be prone to racking and too short to find much use. That, plus the fact that I simply like the idea of a hidden drawer, led me to put a drawer on the end of this table. The drawer on my table is on the right end, but you could switch it to the left end if that makes more sense for the spot where your table will live.

The drawer itself is set in a fairly traditional drawer opening – it's just sideways. A stretcher below the drawer is tenoned into the table legs and wraps around the legs. The stretcher above the drawer also wraps around the legs but is secured to the legs from above with a single dovetail. If you've never used this technique, it's much easier than you

The stretcher above the drawer is marked to length, notched and dovetailed. The dovetail is then transferred to the top of the leg. The bulk of the dovetail slot is routed out, then chiseled to fit.

might imagine. Just cut the tails on the stretcher and then knife the outline of the dovetail directly onto the table leg. To get a flat bottom on the dovetailed slot in the legs, I use a $1/8$" straight bit to rout out the bulk of the waste. Then I fine-tune the dovetail slot with chisels.

Before assembling the base, cut small mortises (mine are $3/16$" thick) on the upper and lower drawer stretchers, as well as on the side apron, to accept tenons cut on the ends of the drawer runners and kicker.

After a quick dry-fit, you're ready to glue up the sides. When the glue has had time to cure, do another thorough dry-fit to make sure that the joints on the front and back apron close up completely. Once you're satisfied with the fit, glue the front and rear apron, as well as the runners and kicker, to the assembled sides.

Build the Tabletop

I used a mitered frame on the perimeter of the tabletop because the look fits the contemporary feel of this design. I typically reinforce my miters with splines or keys, but for a sleeker, cleaner look I used loose tenons to join this frame.

When choosing stock for the cherry frame, look for straight grain for the straight pieces and use a piece with arched grain to match the curve on the front piece of the frame. Start by cutting the three straight parts of the frame to size. Leave the front piece of the frame oversized and square at this point – it

makes cutting the angle on the end much easier.

The joints at the back of the tabletop are mitered at 45°, which can be done at the table saw or on your miter saw. The angle on the front joints can be pulled off the full-sized drawing using a bevel gauge and transferring the angle to your table saw or miter saw.

Before moving on, take time to test the fit of all the joints and make sure they close completely. To tweak them for a perfect fit I use a piece of sandpaper glued to a flat scrap of wood. Once you're satisfied with the fit, band saw and fair the curve on the front piece.

To mortise for the loose tenons I used a plunge router outfitted with a straight bit and guide fence, as shown on page 97. Place the mortises so that the joints won't poke through the edges of the frame or panel groove. Once the mortises are done, cut the loose tenons to thickness and width at the table saw. Then round over the edges and cut them to length. To house the bird's-eye maple panel in the tabletop, use the router table to mill a $1/4$"-wide × $1/2$"-deep groove centered on the inside edges of all four frame members. On the inner top edges of the frame pieces, mill a $3/16$" × $3/16$" chamfer.

Having glued up the curved front apron, veneering the flat panel is easy. I used the same vacuum bag setup and used bird's-eye maple veneer on the top and plain maple veneer on the bottom. For the core of my panel, I used $3/8$" MDF

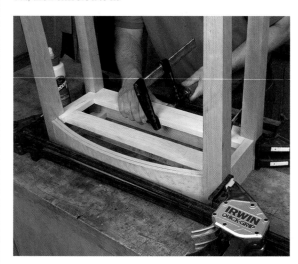

Clamp up the long aprons and add the drawer runners and kicker. Runners and the kicker are tenoned at both ends. The rear runner is also glued to the rear apron.

The assembled base is outfitted with drawer runners, a kicker and guides. The false drawer front looks like an apron when the drawer is closed – you can't even tell it's there.

Clamp scrap stock flush to the ends of the frame members to steady the router and use double-sided tape to a guide fence on your router base. Then take plunge cuts until you reach full mortise depth.

Plane and rip stock to fit the mortises in the frame members of the tabletop. Then round over the edges at the router table and trim the tenons to length.

To make sure the tabletop goes together square and flat, use a quickly made and self-squaring assembly jig that allows you to register two adjacent sides off of right-angle guides.

because I had it on hand, but a quality plywood would work, too.

Rabbet the bottom edge of the panel. Before you glue up the top, apply a few coats of finish to the panel. I like to glue up tabletops or any flat assembly on an assembly jig made from a piece of $\frac{3}{4}$"-thick melamine to which I've screwed two guide boards at a right angle. After applying glue, I butt adjacent flat frame parts against the guide boards. For the curved front piece of the frame I cut a few scraps to match the curve. Once clamps are applied to close up the joint, make sure the tabletop is flat to the melamine. If it's not, add a few clamps to hold it down.

To give the table a lighter feel and a sense of lift, I routed a $\frac{3}{8}$" × $\frac{3}{8}$" chamfer on the bottom edge of the top.

Add a Drawer & Finish

The drawer can be made in whatever fashion you prefer. I dovetailed a simple maple box and installed a cherry drawer bottom just to add a little contrast. Once the drawer is built and fitted, using a false drawer front allows you to size it for a piston-tight fit between the legs.

I routed a cove on the inside edge at the bottom of the false drawer front so I can reach underneath and open it easily. A nice touch for the hidden drawer would be a hidden locking mechanism, such as one of those that Charles Bender

wrote about in his article "It's a Secret" (popularwoodworking.com/nov09).

Though I finished the panel on the tabletop prior to assembly, I still sand the frame and lay on a few more coats of Waterlox before attaching it to the base, to build the sheen and lend more protection. The base of this table got three coats of finish, and the top got about six. Before the final coat, I wet-sand the entire piece with #600-grit wet-dry sandpaper, apply a thick coat and then wipe it nearly dry after a few minutes.

To attach the top to the base, I screwed directly through the drawer kicker and into both the top panel and the sides of the tabletop frame. To allow the front and back of the tabletop to expand and contract just a little, I used figure-8 tabletop fasteners to secure it in place and prevent warping.

It's a satisfying build and a handsome little table. The contrast of the cherry surrounding the bird's-eye maple panel and aprons serves to highlight the beauty of the veneer. And the drawer is a nice surprise – one you can keep to yourself or show off to your friends.

4 Ways to Build a Tavern Table

BY TROY SEXTON

We used to have a table just like this one that was great for playing cards or board games with our two kids. Unfortunately, I sold that table and have always regretted it. So when we finished out a couple new basement rooms for the kids, building a new game table was first on my list.

The top of this table is made from three boards of wormy chestnut, a species of wood that you're going to have to hunt for. I bought mine from a wholesaler who bought it out of a barn in the Smokies. And it was expensive: about $10 a board foot. The painted base is made from poplar.

Begin the project by milling the legs and cutting the taper. You can use a tapering jig for your table saw, but I don't recommend it. A few years ago I came up with a quick way to use a jointer to cut tapers faster and safer. See the story on this technique on page 103.

There are a lot of ways you can join the aprons to the legs, from totally traditional to quick-and-dirty. I prefer using a straight mortise-and-tenon joint, though if I were building a little side table or something else that wouldn't see daily abuse, the two less traditional methods I'm going to cover would work just fine. But before we talk about the bases, build the top.

Making the Top

After I pulled the right boards from my woodpile, I got them ready for glue-up. I wanted this top to look rustic, so I didn't plane the lumber. Instead, I jointed the edges of the planks and glued up the top. Then I rough sanded it with a belt sander to get it reasonably flat and to remove some of the milling marks. Then I cut the top to size and worked on the breadboard ends.

For a long time I used traditional through-mortises to attach breadboards to cover the end grain of my tabletops. Other people showed me how to do it with slotted screw holes. I was always against using that method until I actually tried it. Now it's the only way I'll attach breadboards. You actually get less up-and-down movement using screws, and the top stays flatter-looking for a longer time. Here's how I make my breadboard ends.

After cutting the breadboards to size, cut $3/8$"-wide by $2^{1}/2$"-long by $1^{1}/2$"-deep mortises in the breadboards. I cut five of these for my 36"-wide top. However many you use, it's always good practice to use an odd number of mortises so it's easier to lay them out. I put the two outside mortises $1/2$" in from the end of the breadboard.

Now cut two slots for two screws in each mortise. I make the slots about $3/8$" long to give the top some real room to move if it has to. You can make a router jig to cut the slots, or you can use your drill press and work the bit back and forth. Clamp the breadboard to the tabletop and put two screws in each mortise. I put the screws at the sides of the mortise, not at the center. I do this because I peg the fake plug later in the process, and this keeps me from boring a hole into one of my screws accidentally. Don't drive the screws in too tightly because you want the tabletop to be able to move.

Now plug the mortises. I cut plugs to fit the opening and taper them a bit so they fit snugly when tapped in place. Glue the plugs in place, then peg the

plugs through the top with $1/4$" × $1/4$" square pegs.

Now age the top. I strike the top with a key ring full of keys; I even write people's names in the top with a knife. It's pretty amusing to watch people as they see me do this. They freak out.

Stain the top with a golden oak color and then add a natural oil finish, such as Watco, which is an oil/varnish blend. You don't want the top to look too shiny.

Now turn your attention to the base.

Mortise & Tenon

Cut your aprons to size. Cut 1"-long tenons that are $3/8$" thick. The apron lengths in the Schedule of Materials include the tenons. I cut my tenons first and use them to lay out my mortises,

I usually build my tables using straight mortise-and-tenon joinery. However, there are special cases when other methods are just as good or even better.

The plugs for the breadboard ends are made from the same material as the tabletop. Sand the plug to fit, put some glue on the sides and tap it in place.

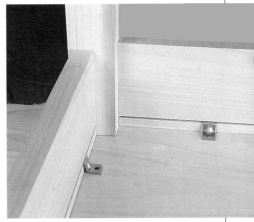

These tabletop fasteners are cheap ($2.99 for a pack of eight) and sturdy. Simply place the clip end into the kerf in your apron and screw the other end to your tabletop.

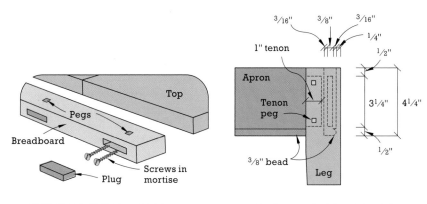

BREADBOARD ENDS DETAIL

3/16"   3/8"   3/16"

1/4"

1" tenon

1/2"

Apron

Tenon
peg

3 1/4"   4 1/4"

3/8" bead

Leg

1/2"

MORTISE AND TENON DETAIL

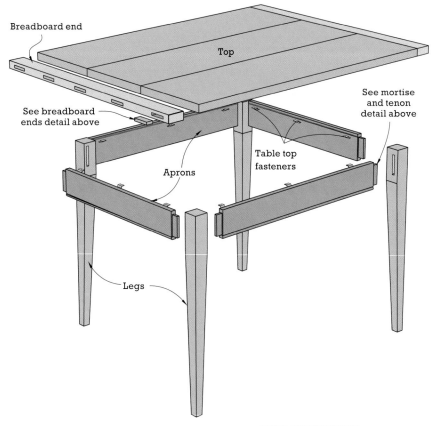

Breadboard end

Top

See breadboard
ends detail above

See mortise
and tenon
detail above

Aprons

Table top
fasteners

Legs

EXPLODED VIEW

which results in less layout, in my opinion. These aprons are set back 1/4" from the front of the legs (this is called a "set back").

Now cut a bead on the bottom edge of the aprons using a beading bit in your router. Finally, cut a slot on the inside of the aprons for fastening the base to the top. I use metal tabletop fasteners from Rockler (see the "Supplies" box on page 103). Rockler sells very sturdy ones, and I recommend them.

For these fasteners, the slot needs to be the width of your table saw's blade (between 1/8" or 1/16" wide) and 7/16" down from the top of the apron and 3/8" deep.

Glue up your base, peg the mortises through the legs and finish the base. I use square pegs in my legs. Drill a round hole through the leg and into the mortise. Then take a piece of square stock, whittle one end of it roundish, then pound it into the hole. It should convert your round hole into a square.

Mitered Mortise & Tenon

This method is similar to the straight mortise and tenon above, but you must miter the ends of the tenons because your mortises meet in the middle of the leg. Why would they meet? Well you might have a thinner leg, or your mortises might be back farther if you chose to use a larger set back.

When this is the case, I make a standard tenon and chop the end off at a 45° angle on my miter saw. You're not trying to match the two miters exactly (it will never show), so leave a little gap between the two tenons. If it's too tight, it could get you in trouble because the ends of the tenons will touch before the shoulders seat into the legs.

Tavern Table

NO.	ITEM	DIMENSIONS (INCHES)			MATERIAL
		T	W	L	
4	Legs	2 1/8	2 1/8	28 1/4	Poplar
2	Aprons*	3/4	4 1/4	31 3/4	Poplar
2	Aprons*	3/4	4 1/4	25 3/4	Poplar
1	Top	1 1/8	36	43	Chestnut
2	Breadboards	1 1/8	2 1/2	36	Chestnut

*Including 1" tenon

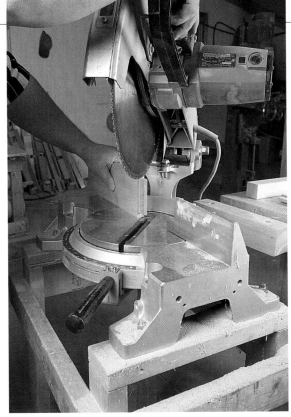

Mitered mortise-and-tenon joinery is common on tables with thin legs or when your set back is deeper than normal.

When you have to use mitered mortise-and-tenon joinery, don't get too worked up about the fit of the miter. You don't want the miter too tight.

Some Thoughts on Table Design

No matter which construction method you use to build your table, there are a few rules you must follow when designing your table. Otherwise your family and guests will be uncomfortable, they'll ram into each other or they'll constantly bang their knees on your aprons.

We've combed several books on the topic of tables and most sources agree on these guidelines.

Table Height • You don't have a lot of room to wiggle here. Make sure your table height falls between $28^{1}/_{2}$" and 30". A few sources state that 32" is OK, but 30" or less is more common.

Apron Height • Make sure each of your sitters has at least 24" to 25" of room between the bottom of the apron and the floor. This means that a 30"-high table with a $^{7}/_{8}$"-thick top should have aprons no wider than $5^{1}/_{8}$".

Overhang • The distance from the edge of the top to the apron can vary. Between 10" and 18" is great – if possible.

Elbow Room • The amount of tabletop allowed for each place setting should be no less than 23". A roomier table will have 28" to 30".

Tabletop Width • The standard width is between 30" and 34". A square table for four should be about 40" × 40". Six can be accommodated by a 60" × 30" top.

Circular Tops • To seat four, make your top 44" in diameter ($34^{1}/_{2}$" per person). To seat six people, make it 54" in diameter ($28^{1}/_{4}$" per person).

Leg Taper • Tapered legs are a common feature of dining tables. Legs should taper down to half their width at the floor. The taper should begin about 1" below the apron.

Sources

For more about standard furniture sizes and basic furniture construction, check out the following books:
• *Illustrated Cabinetmaking* by Bill Hylton, Fox Chapel Publishing, ISBN #978-1-56-523369-0
• *Measure Twice, Cut Once* by Jim Tolpin, Popular Woodworking Books, ISBN #978-1-55-870809-9

Pocket Screws

I wouldn't recommend this for a large table. If you're going to spend the money on the wood, you might as well do it right. But if you want to build a quick-and-dirty side table, this will work fine. Be sure to glue and screw this joint for added strength. It's important to keep the pieces tightly together as you screw the apron to the leg.

Corner Brackets

Corner brackets are a faster alternative to traditional joinery, but they aren't as sturdy. However, you can't beat them when you want to make a table that can be knocked down and stored away.

These measurements apply to the brackets from Rockler (see the "Supplies" box on page 103). The first step to installing these brackets is to cut a bevel on the inside corner of the legs. This is where you'll later install the hanger bolts. The best way to cut the bevel is on your jointer. Set the machine's fence to a 45° angle and the depth of cut to ¼". Cut 3½" in on the top corner as shown in the bottom left photo on the next page.

Now install the hanger bolts, which are odd-looking fasteners that have wood screw threads on one end and machine screw threads on the other. The wood screw end goes into the leg, and the machine screw end is bolted to the corner bracket. To install the hanger bolts, first lay out and drill pilot holes on the leg. Then install the bolts using the method shown in the bottom left photo on the next page.

Now you need to cut a kerf in each apron for the bracket to grab. The kerf should be 1¾" in from the end and ⅜" deep for these brackets. Different brands can use different measurements.

Attaching the Top & Finishing

I attach the top with tabletop fasteners that I screw in place about every foot. On the long aprons, don't push the fasteners all the way into the kerf when screwing them down. This will give your top some room to move.

I finished the base with a couple coats of latex paint followed by a glazing stain. Finally, I added a couple coats of lacquer for protection.

Be sure to glue the joint and hold the leg and apron together tightly while screwing it together.

Pocket screws aren't my first choice for building dining tables, but for a small occasional table, it'll work.

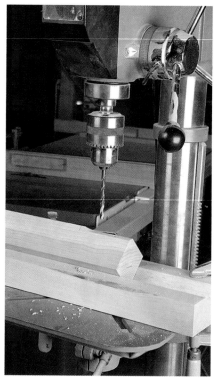

Use the bracket as a template for locating the holes for the corner bracket. Then use a drill press to make your pilot holes.

If You Have a Jointer, Throw Your Tapering Jig Away

For years I used a tapering jig on my table saw to cut tapers on legs. Even after cutting hundreds of the things, I never liked using the jig. It felt unsafe and always brought my fingers too close to the blade for comfort. One day this method came to me out of the blue. It works so well and so fast that I'm still kicking myself for not thinking of it sooner. It uses your jointer and can cut just about any taper in only two quick passes.

Let me show you how to do this on a $2^1/8$" × $2^1/8$" × $28^1/4$" leg. First, mark on the leg where the apron will be. Let's say the apron is 4" wide. Add 1" to that and make a mark 5" down from the top of the leg. Then take the remainder of the leg, $23^1/4$", divide that number in half and forget about the fraction – so you get 11". Make a mark on the leg that's 11" up from the bottom of the leg. To reduce the width of the leg at the floor by half (which is standard with leg tapering), set your jointer to make a $1/2$"-deep cut. Now make your first pass on the jointer by slowly pushing the leg into the cutterhead – foot first – until you reach the mark at 11". Lift the leg off the jointer.

Now turn the leg around so the top part is headed towards the cutterhead. Place your pusher-holddown block on the bottom of the leg and push down so you "pop a wheelie" with your leg. Slowly push the leg into the cutterhead while pushing down and forward on your pusher-holddown block. When you finish this pass you will have a perfectly tapered leg on one side.

Here I am making the first pass on the leg. My jointer is set to make a $1/2$"-deep cut. As soon as the cutterhead reaches the mark at 11", pull the leg up off the jointer.

Here I'm beginning the second pass on the jointer. I've turned the leg around and "popped a wheelie" using my pusher-holddown block. Advance slowly and steadily into the cutterhead.

Here I am near the end of the second pass. The outfeed table supports the tapered side after it comes off the cutterhead, so the leg moves steadily over the jointer beds as long as I keep firm pressure down on the pusher-holddown block.

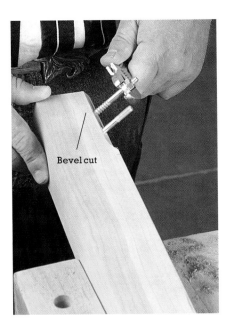

To install the hanger bolts, thread two machine nuts onto the end of the hanger bolt and tighten them against one another. Then grip the two nuts with a wrench and screw the hanger bolts into the leg.

Corner brackets are great for building furniture that needs to be knocked down or moved frequently.

Supplies

Rockler
rockler.com or 800-279-4441

3" × $4^3/4$" corner brackets, set of 4, item #34303, $5.59

Table top fasteners, 8 per pack, item #34215, $2.99

Prices as of publication date.

Building Extension Tables

BY TROY SEXTON

If you've served one too many turkey dinners with your aunts and uncles huddled around a card table, then it's time to build a dining table with extension leaves.

By using commercially available table slides and legs, it's a project that's not much more difficult than building an end table. There are merely a few extra details that you need to watch out for as you go.

The table shown here will accommodate up to 10 people when extended to its full 100" length. It's basically a Queen Anne design that uses a cabriole leg with a pad foot. But the plan and procedure that follows can be used for any style or size extension table. When you visit the web sites listed in the "Supplies" box on page 108, you'll see how easy it is to customize your table to fit almost any furniture style by choosing different legs and altering the apron just a bit.

Begin With the Aprons

The aprons on the table are $4^{1}/4$" wide with small knee brackets glued on the ends to act as a transition into the curve on the legs. (Many of the other styles of legs available for sale will not need a transitional detail on the apron.)

When making the aprons, the first thing to do is to cut the tenons on the ends. The tenons measure $3/8$" thick, $3^{1}/4$" wide and 1" long. I cut mine using a dado stack and a miter gauge on my table saw. To cut the face cheeks and shoulders, set the height of the dado stack to $3/16$" and the fence at 1" from the left-most blade in your dado stack.

To cut the edge shoulders and cheeks on the tenons, raise the height of the dado stack to $1/2$" and leave the fence at 1". Test the fit of your tenons in a sample mortise cut using your hollow-chisel mortiser, plunge router or chisel.

With the tenons cut, glue $3/4$" × 2" × $4^{1}/2$" blocks on the edges at the ends of the aprons. Try to match the grain and color of the blocks and aprons as best you can. When the glue is dry, use a band saw or jigsaw to cut the detail shown in the diagram on page 107 and sand the edges smooth.

Now is the time to prepare your aprons to attach them to the top. It might be tempting to use commercial Z-shaped

Cut the knee brackets on the ends of the aprons using your band saw (top). Then clean up the cuts using a drum sander in your drill press (right).

clips (also called tabletop fasteners). While I've used this hardware for all sorts of tables, it has been my experience that it isn't well-suited for use with extension tables. Here's why: When you install the clips, you need to leave a little expansion room between the tongue of the clip and the bottom of the groove you cut in the long aprons. This space allows the table to expand and contract with the seasons. What I've found is that these clips can also allow the top to shift or skew, especially if the top gets knocked. If this happens, you won't be able to get the holes in the extension leaves to line up with your dowels and the table won't go together unless you loosen the Z-shaped clips and realign all the top pieces.

When I build tables, I prefer to instead use pocket screws every 6" that I ream out slightly using a drill bit to allow the top to move but not shift. Finish sand the aprons and move on to the legs.

Mortising the Legs

Cutting and shaping cabriole legs is a skill unto itself that will test your band

saw, rasping and sanding skills. As a result, even professionals will outsource their legs for a job such as this because the price is quite reasonable and the legs are presanded.

With some leg-making companies you can even pay a little more and they will mortise the legs for you. I have a mortiser, so I saved a few bucks and did it myself. The only tricky aspect of cutting the mortise in cabriole legs is clamping the leg so its curve fits against the fence of your mortising machine. I put the legs up on small blocks of wood for my machine. (If you are making the cabriole legs yourself instead of buying them, cut the mortises before you shape the legs.)

The aprons are set back $3/16$" from the

A self-centering doweling jig (right) makes quick work of drilling the holes for the dowel pins. Just make sure your jig really hits the center of the work – some do not. A little glue is all it takes to secure the pin in its hole.

legs, so your mortises should be located 3/8" from the outside edge of the leg.

Decisions, Decisions

With the mortises cut, it's time to make a decision. Should you glue the table base together and then cut it apart? Or should you crosscut the long aprons first and then glue up each end?

I find it easier to glue and clamp up the base, let it dry and then cut it apart using my chop saw and the help of a couple family members. (If you're building a table this big, you should have a few of them around.)

After the base is glued up, merely mark the midpoint of the aprons, put the table base on your chop saw and make the cut. Have your helpers hold the ends, especially on the second cut when the whole thing comes apart. You're going to be surprised at how easy this is to do.

If that all seems too much, you can make the cut using a circular saw. Or you can cut the aprons before you glue up the mortise-and-tenon joint. If that's your decision, I recommend clamping the aprons you cut apart together using an intermediate board to keep everything square as you glue up the base.

Top & Leaves

Now surface all the lumber for the two top pieces and two leaves. Remember that the leaves will have their grain running perpendicular to the grain in the top. Glue up the panels you need for the top and leave them 2" oversized to make cutting the shape of the top easier. You also should leave the leaves a couple inches too long, too, so they can be cut to fit at the same time as the top.

When the extension leaves are in use in this table, they are kept in the same plane as the top by using dowel pins.

You can buy special dowel pins for extension tables that have a bullet-shaped end. The tapered shape makes them easy to align and slide together. However, I find the pins simple to make using 3/8" dowel stock and sanding the edges to a bullet shape myself.

Begin by drilling the holes for the dowels in both edges of the leaves and the edges of the top pieces. The 3/8"-diameter holes should be 1" deep. Drill five holes in each edge: one in the center, two at 10" from the center and two at 20" from the center.

Glue the 1 7/8"-long pins in place and sand their exposed edge to a bullet shape to make fitting the leaves together easier.

Now put the two top pieces and leaves all together upside down on your bench and lay out the top. After toying with more complex shapes, I settled on a simple top that was 44" wide with half-round

Extension Table

NO.	ITEM	DIMENSIONS (INCHES)			MATERIAL
		T	W	L	
1	Top	3/4	44	76	Cherry
2	Leaves	3/4	12	44	Cherry
4	Aprons for leaves	3/4	4 1/4	12	Cherry
2	Short aprons	3/4	4 1/4	24 1/4	Cherry
2	Long aprons	3/4	4 1/4	54 1/4	Cherry
4	Legs*	1 3/4	1 3/4	29	Cherry
8	Knee brackets	3/4	2	4 1/2	Cherry

*Thickness and width refers to the block at the top of the leg

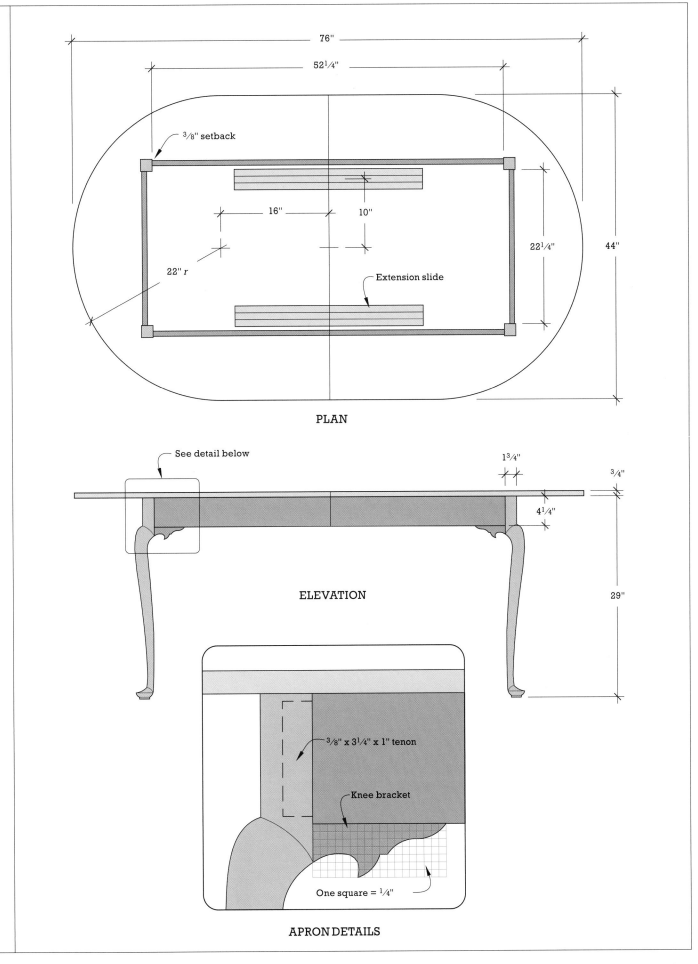

76"

52¹/₄"

³/₈" setback

16"   10"

22¹/₄"

44"

22" r

Extension slide

PLAN

See detail below

1³/₄"

³/₄"

4¹/₄"

29"

ELEVATION

³/₈" x 3¹/₄" x 1" tenon

Knee bracket

One square = ¹/₄"

APRON DETAILS

shapes on the ends that are a 22" radius. This shape is sometimes called a "race-track oval" in furniture circles.

Cut out the shape of the top using your jigsaw. Now put the base in place on the underside of your top and get ready to attach it. As you can see by the photos and cutting list, I added apron pieces to the leaves that match the apron on the table base. These let you use the table fully extended without a tablecloth. Clamp these extra aprons and table base pieces in place on the top and screw everything down tightly.

Using a small punch, I marked a number on the underside of each leaf's edge and the same number at the edge it mates to. This allows the table to look exactly as I intended every time it's set up.

Supplies

You can buy table legs from a variety of excellent sources, including:

Classic Designs by Matthew Burak
tablelegs.com or 800-748-3480

The legs and table slides for this project came from Classic Designs by Matthew Burak, which features a wide range of table legs in a variety of woods. The legs are the Queen Anne Padfoot Dining Table leg, item #100D-CH, which cost $67.95 each. These legs also are available in red oak, soft maple and black walnut. Check the company's web site for prices.

Other styles of table legs available include: Federal, William & Mary and Hepplewhite.

The table slides also came from the same company. The 26" slides are item #51026 and cost $36.95 for a pair.

Other sources for good legs are:

Adams Wood Products
adamswoodproducts.com or 423-587-2942

Osborne Wood Products
osbornewood.com or 800-849-8876

Prices as of publication date.

Extension Hardware

You can make your own table slides using a hardwood such as maple and some sliding dovetail joints. But why would you want to torture yourself this way? You can buy the extensions slides from a variety of sources (see the "Supplies" box below). The set of slides for this table cost $36.95.

Table slides are easy to install; there are just a couple tricks. The first thing you want to be careful of is to install the slides perfectly parallel to each other, with the center of each slide 10" from the center of the tabletop. Also, make sure you are installing the slides right-side up (this should be obvious, but you should check). The slides are bowed slightly to compensate for sagging.

To install the slides, you need to mark parallel lines that show where the inside edge and outside edge of each slide should go. Watch these lines as you position and screw down the slides.

Now extend the slides so they are 50" long and position them between your lines. Whatever you do, don't extend the slides all the way when you install

them because then the leaves cannot be removed. Screw the slides down through the predrilled holes.

Finishing Touches

With the top attached and the table slides working, flip the tabletop onto its legs and begin cleaning up the top's edge with a belt sander to remove the saw-blade marks from your jigsaw. When that looks good, rout a $\frac{5}{8}$" roundover on the top edge using your router. Finally, finish sand the top and edges up to #180 grit using a random-orbit sander.

I dyed the table using a reddish water-based aniline dye that I mixed myself by blending several colors. A good place to find similar dyes is at Woodworker's Supply (woodworker.com or 800-645-9292). Then I followed that up with a couple coats of clear water-based lacquer.

With this table complete, a lot of grown-ups in the Sexton family will now be able to graduate from the "kiddie" table when Thanksgiving rolls around again – maybe even me.

If you don't have a set of trammel points, here's a good trick. Take your straightedge ruler and drill a small hole at 0" and at the dimension of the radius you want (22" in this case). Drawing the half-round end is then a simple matter with a nail and a pencil.

Attaching Solid Wood Tabletops

BY BILL HYLTON

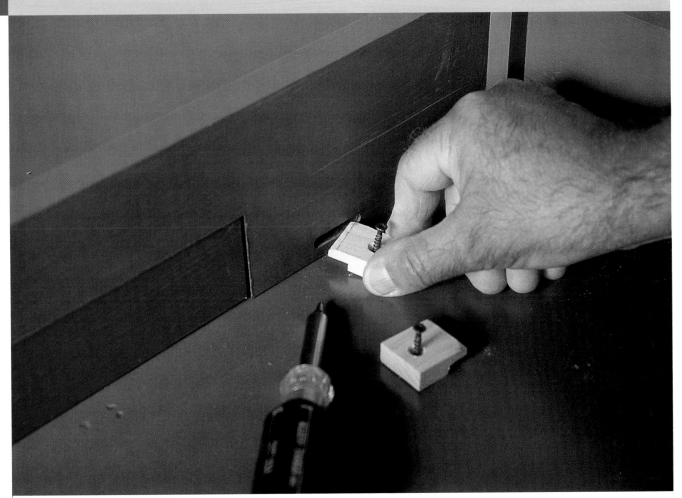

About a decade ago, I made a drop-leaf table for a book of projects. When it came time to mount the top, I just drilled pilot holes and drove cut nails through the top into the aprons. Are you horrified? Actually, the approach worked great. In the years since I put it together, the top has remained sound and firmly affixed to the aprons. And while I don't hesitate to use this approach when the circumstances are right, such as on an informal kitchen table, there are many better ways to mount a tabletop to its stand.

You could attach a tabletop to its stand with blocks glued securely to both the aprons and the tabletop. This doesn't allow the tabletop to expand and contract, of course, and the resulting stresses eventually will split or buckle the top.

And herein is the challenge: how to prevent wood's ongoing expansion and contraction from destroying the assembly or itself. The tabletop must be held

Buttons are but one method for attaching tabletops. Here's how they work: Slip the button's tongue into its groove and screw it to the tabletop. Avoid jamming the button's shoulder tight to the apron. A gap ensures the tabletop's natural movement can be accommodated. Buttons are screwed to the tabletop, not the aprons. But each has a tongue that projects into a groove in the apron, pinching the apron tight to the tabletop.

How do I make those narrow slots, you ask? I bore a hole at each end of the layout, then nibble away the waste between them with the same drill bit. It's not particularly elegant, but it works.

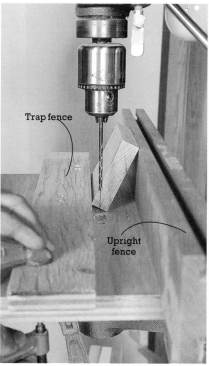

The key to drilling pockets is attitude – that is, the angle of the apron in relation to the bit. Lean the apron against an upright fence, align the pilot layout on the end with a bit in the drill chuck, and trap it at the right angle with a flat fence.

tight to the leg assembly, but in such a way as to allow the top to expand and contract.

Most woodworkers know this, of course, and I think that's why so many of them cringe at the thought of face-nailing a tabletop to its stand. Well OK – it may also be an affront to their aesthetic sensibilities.

To make it a bit easier, let's assume here that the tabletop's grain is square to a rectilinear leg-and-apron stand. That is, two of the aprons are parallel with the tabletop's grain and two are perpendicular to it. The shape of the top – square, rectangular, round, oval, free-form – has no bearing on this. The grain direction, and thus the direction of expansion and contraction, is what's important.

If you're building a table with curved aprons, or no aprons at all, you'll have to extrapolate from my examples to fit your specific design.

Glue & Screw Blocks
An improved version of the glue-block method is to secure blocks or ledger strips to the aprons, then drive screws through them into the tabletop. This is an excellent approach, so long as elongated pilot holes, properly oriented, are used to allow for seasonal expansion and contraction of the wood.

First of all, the grain of the blocks should parallel the apron's grain. Wood movement doesn't have an impact here, so you can glue, nail or screw the blocks to the aprons. But before you do, bore pilots for the screws – you want to use screws, not nails – to secure them to the tabletop.

At the center of the block that runs

cross-grain is a "fixed pilot," a hole matched to the diameter of the screw. This screw anchors the tabletop to the leg assembly; all the movement occurs on either side of this point. Flanking the fixed pilot should be pilot slots that parallel the block's grain.

The blocks that run parallel to the tabletop grain should have only slotted pilot holes, and they must be oriented across the grain.

Making the fixed pilot is, of course, simple. Drill a hole. But making the slots is more of a challenge. Typically, I use a $3/16$" twist drill bit in the drill press. I position the block with a thin (low) fence clamped to the table.

Drill holes to delineate the ends of the slot, then nibble away the waste between them. A twist bit, of course, skitters off the wood into one or the other of the holes, but it doesn't take long to form a trench. Lock the quill and slide the work back and forth along the fence to tidy the slot.

With the right sort of screw, one with a washer-like head, you can use $1/4$"-wide slots, which you can produce easily with a Forstner bit. This is a little less trying than using a twist bit, because a Forstner doesn't wander. Although I'm a dedicated router user, I don't view this as a router job. The diameter and length of bit necessary – $3/16$" to $1/4$" – makes routing an iffy proposition, in my opinion. You also need two setups, one for the cross-grain slots, another for the long-grain ones.

Were I to tackle this as a router job, I'd rout the slots in a wide board, then rip the strips from it. Then I'd lay out the slots and use an edge guide to position the long-grain cuts and guide the router.

Next, use a T-square to guide the cross-grain cuts. Just eyeball the beginning and end of each slot, and make each slot with a series of cuts, each plunged progressively deeper.

Screw Pockets
It's quite common these days to skip the blocks and just drill oversized pilot holes directly in the aprons. You can run long screws straight up through an apron's edge and into the tabletop, or through angled pockets cut in an apron's inside face. The latter approach works better for me, because it lets me use shorter screws.

Creating the pockets and pilots is easiest if you have a pocket jig and related accessories, but it's not the only way.

With a drill press and Forstner bit, you can make very tidy, uniform pockets. Lay out the pocket locations on the apron. Chuck a Forstner bit in the drill press – I usually use a $1/2$" size. Hold the apron at an angle and bore the pocket. The design of the bit enables it to slice cleanly into the wood to form a flat-bottomed pocket.

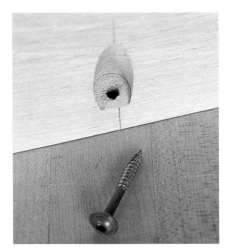

The completed pocket is flat-bottomed and large enough for a screw with an integral washer.

The real trick here is setting and holding the apron at the right angle. You typically see the apron cradled in a nifty custom-made jig. Is such a jig worthwhile for the occasional project? I don't think so. I use two fences: One is upright to lean the apron against, the second is a flat trap fence set against the apron's bottom edge to hold at it the correct angle.

I establish the angle by laying it out on the end of a scrap of the apron stock. I'll usually put a small rule on the scrap's end and draw an eyeballed angle from the center of the edge to a spot $1\frac{1}{2}$" to 2" up the inside face. If you prefer to use a sliding bevel, set it to about 15°.

Chuck a twist bit in the drill press, lower the bit almost to the table, and lock the quill. Line up the layout line with the bit, setting the upright fence so the apron is tilted just right. Then slide the trap fence against the apron to keep the bottom edge from skidding forward and changing the angle. Change to the Forstner bit, set an apron in place, then bore the pockets.

After boring all the pockets, switch back to a twist bit and bore the pilots. Most of these pilots must be elongated, of course, but with pockets, this is usually accomplished by rocking the drill to expand the exit hole. You can't do this on the drill press so switch to a hand drill. Rock the drill parallel to the aprons that will be across the tabletop's grain, and across the aprons that will parallel the grain.

Buttons are Better

And there's yet another solution, and it's one I often use when constructing a table. It uses "buttons" spaced around the tabletop inside the aprons. A button, often called a cabinetmaker's button, is a small block, roughly $1\frac{1}{4}$" square and $\frac{3}{4}$" or less thick. It has a tongue, which you stick into a groove cut in the apron. You then drive a screw through the button body into the tabletop. Over time, as the tabletop expands and contracts, the button moves with it. As it does, the tongue moves along, or in and out of, its groove in the apron.

The apron grooves can be through or stopped. Some use through grooves in the aprons that cross the tabletop grain, because the button's tongue will move along the groove. But they use stopped grooves in the long-grain aprons, figuring that here the tongue is moving in and out. I tend to use stopped grooves all around. I'll divvy up a long apron's length for three or four buttons, but use only a single one in the center of a short apron.

Through grooves can be cut on the table saw or routed with a straight bit or slot cutter. Stopped grooves are a router proposition, or you could use a biscuit joiner.

To ensure the tabletop is held tightly to the stand, design the button so its shoulder is slightly shorter than the space between the apron's top edge and the groove. When screwed to the tabletop, the button should be slightly pitched. The tongue should be slightly thinner than the width of the groove. To accommodate the pitch, you may need to chamfer the tip of the tongue.

First, figure out the thickness of button needed, mill a scrap board, and cut a rabbet across each end. Crosscut a strip about $1\frac{1}{4}$" long from each end, then rip the strips into buttons about 1" wide. Drill a pilot hole through the body of each button.

With any of the attachment methods I've described – glue-and-screw blocks, screws in pockets, buttons – final assembly involves setting the tabletop, show face down, on the bench. You upend the leg-and-apron assembly and align it on the top. Then you drive the mounting screws.

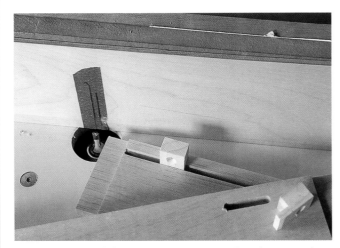

A through-groove is less venturesome to rout than the stopped groove, and requires no layout. A button works in either.

Cut a rabbet across the end of a wide board, then cut off a strip as long as you want the buttons to be. Clip the strip into uniformly sized buttons.

How Tables Work

BY ROBERT W. LANG

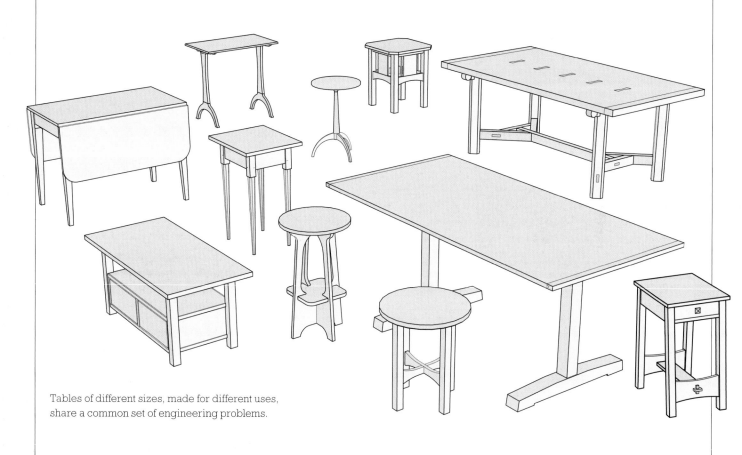

Tables of different sizes, made for different uses, share a common set of engineering problems.

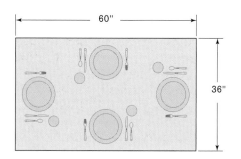

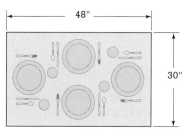

A rule of thumb for seating is to allow 24"–30" per person around the perimeter of the table. But you also must consider the shape and overall size of the table. Extra space is needed at each corner, and while a narrow table may accommodate two settings across from each other, there may not be room for serving dishes in between. There is no substitute for a scaled layout. More examples are online at popularwoodworking.com/apr10.

A good furniture maker is part artist and part engineer. An overemphasis on either side of this equation leads to furniture that is ugly, impractical or both. Tables are especially vulnerable in this regard. Tables serve many purposes and are simpler than cabinets or chairs. But this simplicity calls for a thorough knowledge of how wood works when in the form of a large flat surface and an underlying structure.

Regardless of style, there are many mistakes lying in wait to spoil the plans of the would-be table maker. Whether you are new to the craft and getting ready to make your first occasional table or are more experienced and aiming to build a showpiece for your dining room, there are many aspects of table design that you need to consider.

Shape & Size

The design process begins with establishing practical parameters. A dining table needs to accommodate a certain number of people on a regular basis, and more on special occasions. An end table provides space for a lamp and a beverage, and an entry table may hold a vase, the mail or your keys.

In addition to being the right size for its use, a table must also fit in the available space. Seating 12 for Thanksgiving dinner is a worthy goal, but not at the expense of daily navigation through the dining room.

At this early stage of the process, a scale drawing of the room or a 3-D model in SketchUp will allow you to consider alternatives. Changing your mind at this stage is much easier than it is after you start cutting wood.

If you find it difficult to visualize things on paper or on the computer screen, you can mock up sizes and shapes with cardboard. Put your idea together with packing tape, place it in the room and live with it for a day or two. You don't want to invest the effort to build the real thing only to hear, "I didn't realize it would be like that" from someone you love when you're done.

Consider also how shapes play a role. Rectangles are easy shapes to make, but sharp corners are painful reminders of too much table in too little space.

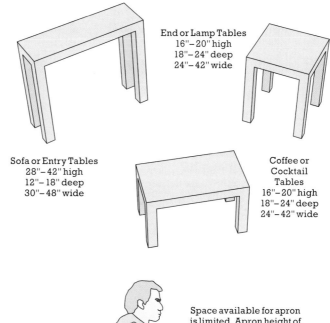

End or Lamp Tables
16"–20" high
18"–24" deep
24"–42" wide

Sofa or Entry Tables
28"–42" high
12"–18" deep
30"–48" wide

Coffee or Cocktail Tables
16"–20" high
18"–24" deep
24"–42" wide

This range of sizes for occasional tables is only a guideline; there are no laws in furniture design.

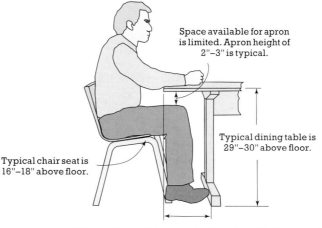

Space available for apron is limited. Apron height of 2"–3" is typical.

Typical chair seat is 16"–18" above floor.

Typical dining table is 29"–30" above floor.

Balance the need to support end of table with clearance for feet. 10"–12" minimum, 16"–18" ideal.

Dining tables and desks don't leave much room for experimentation. If in doubt, pull up a chair and grab a yardstick.

Rounded shapes are more adaptable if you need to squeeze in an extra diner or two, but will be more demanding to build. Clipping square corners will protect your hips or shins if you need to make the most of a tight space.

For dining tables, a simple ratio of human body to perimeter space rarely works. Consider the available space at corners or across the table, and how that affects the table's function. The drawings above give some examples.

Perfect the plan first, then work on establishing the proper height for the structural elements. Standard heights have evolved over the years for the distance from floor to tabletop for different types of tables. You may want to vary the height to suit your needs, but consider the consequences. Restaurants often provide tables an odd height to make people uncomfortable so they won't linger.

Desks and dining tables must also be able to accommodate a chair, and the person on the chair, with enough room between the table and wall to get in and out. Compare what you are considering to existing designs, and spend a few minutes with a yardstick, a folding chair and a card table and you'll find out if the dimensions you're considering will work in real life.

Start on Top

With the overall parameters of size and shape established, stylistic and structural details are next in line. Here is where the balance between structure and style is most important. As you develop your plan, consider the forces that will be working against you. Considerations one and two are movement of the top, and leverage on the ends of the legs.

A solid-wood top will move across the

grain as the seasons change. Moisture (or the lack of it) in the air will migrate to (or from) the top and it will change in width. The number of variables involved makes predicting how much change will take place a guessing game, but it will happen. This is a force that you can't control, but you can design around it.

In most table designs, the top and the base are individual units that work together. The connection between the two must be strong, with some provision for the top to shrink and swell. Cabinetmaker's buttons and figure-8 fasteners are time-tested solutions. If someone suggests a method to you that includes the phrase, "that will keep it from moving," be aware that you are listening to a fool.

Wood movement can't be controlled, but it can be directed. In a dining table you can screw the top to the base in the center and use sliding fasteners on the perimeter to let the top move equally toward each long edge. On a desk, you can use a solid connection at the front edge to maintain appearances and force the results of the movement to the back.

In most tables, the wood grain will be in line with the longest dimension of the table. If you want an attractive table, use the widest material you can find and arrange the individual boards for the most attractive appearance. Historically, tables were made this way without suffering any dire results.

The common advice to use narrow strips and to alternate the direction of growth rings may have some merit if you're operating a large factory, using

suspect material and a finish that will take the life out of the wood. If you're carefully making one table at a time, this procedure will lead you to do more work than necessary to produce an ugly table.

Use the best material you can find for the top. It will be the prominent visual feature of your table, and bad decisions during construction will haunt you forever. I make tops first so I can pick the best material from what I have available, and I usually spend more time finding the right pieces to put together than I spend in actual fabrication.

Match the color and grain patterns, and arrange the boards for appearance. You can overcome surfacing problems by adjusting tools and techniques, but you won't be able to change ugly. Let the wood acclimate to your shop and carefully mill each piece as flat and as straight as you can. Establish a flat surface for gluing to minimize the work you need to do on the assembled top.

Breadboard ends look nice, but their ability to keep a top flat is overstated. You won't be able to straighten out a large warped piece of wood with a skinny straight one. In addition to attaching the breadboard to the top with a tongue and groove, add three or five tenons. The tenon in the center is the only one that should be glued. Allow room for move-

ment in the outer mortises, and use pegs to hold the joint tight. Get used to the fact that the only time you will see the end of the breadboard flush with the edge of the top will be the day you make it.

A Sound Structure

The most common type of support structure is four legs connected by aprons. This design has been used for centuries, but there are weak points. As long as a table is sitting still, skinny legs and aprons are fine. Put some pressure on the bottom of the leg, however (think of dragging a heavy table or kicking a leg as you pass by), and there is enough leverage to break apart the joints or the wood around them.

Mortise-and-tenon joints offer the strongest connection, but two aprons intersecting a leg at a right angle introduce complications, especially if the legs are narrow. Rules based on making a framed panel won't apply for the size and location of the tenons.

Size the elements of the joints so that plenty of material remains around the mortises. Tenons don't have to be centered on an apron's thickness; they can be offset if need be. The longer the tenon the better, and mitering the ends of tenons that would otherwise intersect gains additional length.

Dominos, dowels and biscuits are easy alternatives for mortises and tenons, but won't be as strong or last as long. Of the three, Dominos are the most durable

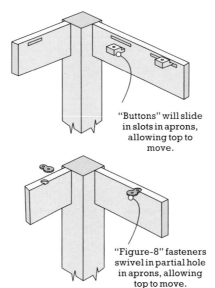

"Buttons" will slide in slots in aprons, allowing top to move.

"Figure-8" fasteners swivel in partial hole in aprons, allowing top to move.

Attach the top to the base structure with a method that allows the top to expand and contract with fluctuations in humidity.

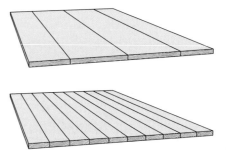

If you want an attractive top, use the widest boards available and arrange them for appearance (top). Gluing tops from many thin strips with alternating end grain is often presented as good technique. In reality, it is more work, with more opportunities for failure – and it makes an ugly top (bottom).

Wood movement can't be stopped, but it can be accommodated. When attaching a top to a base, use fasteners that will slide or swivel.

30"

alternative as they most closely approximate a mortise-and-tenon joint. Biscuits should be used in pairs to maximize the meat of the joint. Dowels may seem strong enough in the short term, but over time either the dowels or the holes for them will move out of round and the joints will fail.

A brace at a 45° angle between the aprons and behind the leg will not be seen and will add support to smaller pieces. These braces can be made of wood as seen in the drawing on the bottom right, and held in place with screws or other joinery. There are also a variety of metal brackets available that serve the same purpose.

Even the best joinery won't eliminate the effects of leverage. The addition of rails and stretchers near the bottom of the legs will form a stronger base, but the trade-off is in both appearance and in use. More structure equals a heavier appearance and interferes with legroom.

On a desk or worktable, rails and stretchers may not be a problem, but in dining tables this can be an issue. Horizontal parts near the floor make inviting footrests and are areas where wear will quickly show.

Connecting rails can be like aprons running from leg to leg, or they can connect pairs of legs. These rails are then connected to each other by a stretcher running the length of the table. A third method is to join the legs from corner to corner, with the cross pieces joined to each other in the center.

The best joint to use is a mortise-and-tenon, but there are alternatives. A single

dovetail is effective for rails that join legs at the top of the leg. This allows the rail to be thin, and the wedge shape of the dovetail resists the outward movement of the legs. Sliding dovetails are traditionally used on small stands to join legs to a central pedestal.

On a Pedestal

There are alternatives to placing a leg on each corner. Tables that are square or circular can be supported by legs attached to a central post. Keep the footprint as

Glue the central mortise and peg the outer mortises to accommodate the cross-grain construction.

Breadboard ends might help keep a top from warping; they also might keep elephants away. If you use them, take care to attach them solidly.

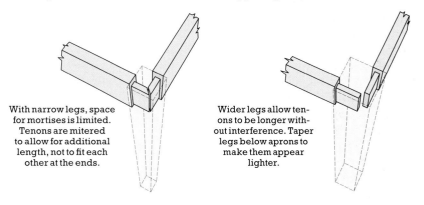

Force applied to the end of a typical table leg generates leverage on the joints above.

Rails and stretchers counteract leverage, but interfere with legroom.

Table legs make excellent levers if there is no supporting structure near the bottom end.

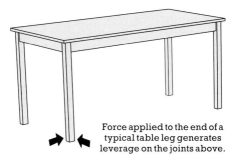

With narrow legs, space for mortises is limited. Tenons are mitered to allow for additional length, not to fit each other at the ends.

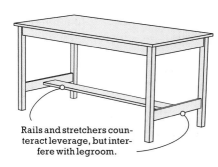

Wider legs allow tenons to be longer without interference. Taper legs below aprons to make them appear lighter.

Narrow legs leave little room for joinery. Mitering the ends increases the length of the tenons; there should be a gap between them where they meet.

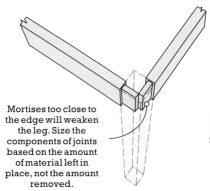

Mortises too close to the edge will weaken the leg. Size the components of joints based on the amount of material left in place, not the amount removed.

How much material is left around a joint is just as important as the size of the joint. Don't put strong tenons in weak legs.

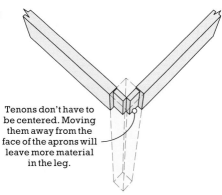

Tenons don't have to be centered. Moving them away from the face of the aprons will leave more material in the leg.

Moving tenons to the back face of a rail is one method to avoid a weak area around a tenon.

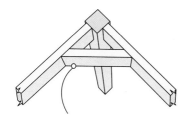

Braces across corners provide additional strength with thin legs and aprons. Metal brackets are available that can simplify this joint.

No one that matters will ever look behind the legs and under the top. Add a wood or metal brace behind the corner if you need to.

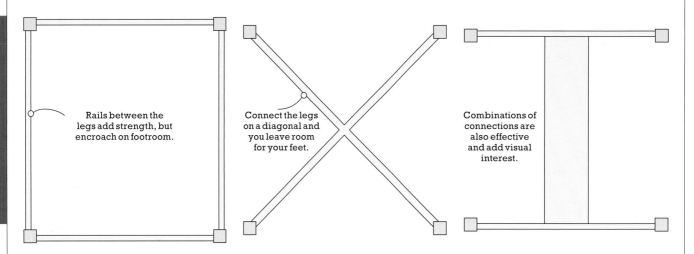

Rails between the legs add strength, but encroach on footroom.

Connect the legs on a diagonal and you leave room for your feet.

Combinations of connections are also effective and add visual interest.

Look for a way to secure the legs without interfering with your feet.

large as is practical to prevent the table from tipping if weight is placed on one end. Imagine the ends of the feet to be vertical legs to get an idea of how they will act in their supporting role.

In small pedestal tables, such as the iconic Shaker candlestand, the legs attach to the pedestal with sliding dovetails. In commercially made dining tables, the typical connection is with hanger bolts in the ends of the feet, held firm with nuts on the inside of a hollow post.

At the top of a pedestal table, a plate wider than the column is used as an intermediate connection for the top. With small tables the connection to the column can be a permanent joint. For larger tables, it's better to use screws or hanger bolts, down to the column and up to the tabletop.

To make a dining table extend, leave a few inches of space between the base and the top for an extension-slide mechanism. In most extension tables, the grain direction is rotated 90° to run across the table. This avoids making an end-to-end match where the two halves join. A side-to-side match will be less obvious when the table is closed.

While you could make your own slides, buying manufactured ones has advantages. There is a lot of engineering and fitting involved in making a slide that will work predictably for an extensive period of time.

Two types of slides are available: one for pedestal tables and one for tables with legs. The type for pedestal tables includes a gear mechanism that equalizes the

movement from the center outward. The two types are also crowned in opposite directions to compensate for sagging as the table is opened. Equalized slides raise slightly at each end in the open position, and the other raises slightly in the center. When the leaves are in place, the surface will be level.

Get the hardware (or at least the actual sizes) first and engineer the table around it, with the appropriate space between the base and the top. Attach the slides with screws to the top and to the structure below. If your extension design incorporates an apron, attach the apron to the top. The joint in the apron will likely open as the top moves seasonally. A small piece of trim to cover the gap, attached to one apron only, is a common fix.

The aggregate width of the leaves should be a couple inches less than the

opening range of the slides. Short dowels with dome-shaped ends will fit the leaves to each other, and to the tabletop.

On the Beam

Feet can also be placed laterally, and connected by posts and beams to make a trestle table. This time-tested alternative to four legs can simplify joinery and make maximum use of minimal amounts of material. Trestle tables are essentially a series of connected I-beams.

Each end has an obvious "I" shape, but looking down on the structure in plan view reveals that the two ends connected by central rails also form an "I." The top in this scheme often plays a structural role, connecting the outer ends of the upper beams, thus keeping the post-and-beam assemblies at each end from twisting or racking.

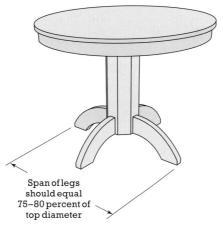

Span of legs should equal 75–80 percent of top diameter

A central column with three or four feet is often a good solution in a limited space.

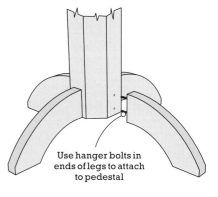

Use hanger bolts in ends of legs to attach to pedestal

In factory-made tables, legs bolt on to a hollow pedestal. Small pedestals often connect the legs to the post with sliding dovetails.

Hybrid structures are often seen, and are a good creative outlet. You can have a trestle form at the base and conventional aprons at the top. Whatever the form, keep an eye on the structural elements. You want the table to be strong and attractive, and you don't want wood movement of the top causing problems.

Structural elements will have an impact on the appearance of the table. Elements associated with specific styles can look odd if placed inappropriately. The proportions of the elements will also impact the overall proportions and appearance of the final design. Tapers, bevels and curves can make parts appear smaller or thinner than they really are.

The last illustration at the bottom of the page shows an unfortunate, but common combination of design mistakes. For a design to look good, it has to make sense, and ignoring hundreds of years of techniques isn't wise. Learn the basics and build on a firm foundation – then get creative.

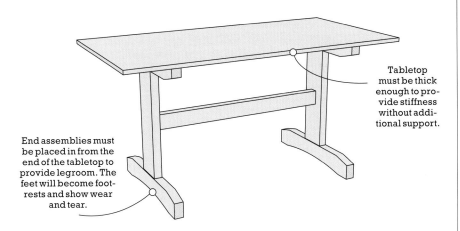

Tabletop must be thick enough to provide stiffness without additional support.

End assemblies must be placed in from the end of the tabletop to provide legroom. The feet will become footrests and show wear and tear.

Trestle tables are another alternative to four legs. Trestles provide a strong structure with a small amount of wood.

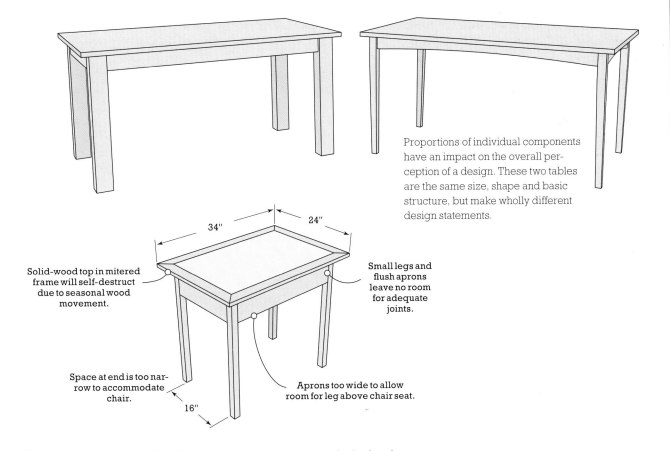

Proportions of individual components have an impact on the overall perception of a design. These two tables are the same size, shape and basic structure, but make wholly different design statements.

34"   24"

Solid-wood top in mitered frame will self-destruct due to seasonal wood movement.

Small legs and flush aprons leave no room for adequate joints.

Space at end is too narrow to accommodate chair.

16"

Aprons too wide to allow room for leg above chair seat.

Table design isn't always intuitive. The drawing above shows several mistakes that beginning table builders tend to make.

A Good Example

If you've never made a table before, or if you just need to exercise your table-building muscles, this small Shaker side table, featured in Issue 2 of *Woodworking Magazine* (Autumn 2004), is a good practice piece. The proportions are excellent, the joinery is sound and it won't require a large investment in materials or time. When you're done you will have an attractive end table or nightstand.

The top is 18" square and connects to the frame with screws in oversized holes in the upper drawer guides. If you choose not to include the drawer, simply repeat the joints from the back aprons at the front and attach the top to the top edge of the aprons.

Starting with a good example is also a good way to practice developing your own designs. One secret to becoming a good designer is to study many different existing forms and experiment with them. Design is a skill that can be learned through practice; it isn't a gift that some of us have and some of us don't.

A SketchUp model of this table is available as a free download at popularwoodworking.com/sketchup. If you have SketchUp installed on your computer, you can download the model and view it in three dimensions to see how it goes together, or you can use the model as a starting point for designing a similar table of a different size.

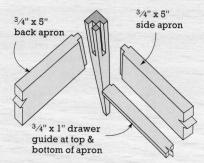

³/₄" x 5" back apron

³/₄" x 5" side apron

³/₄" x 1" drawer guide at top & bottom of apron

BACK LEG JOINT DETAILS

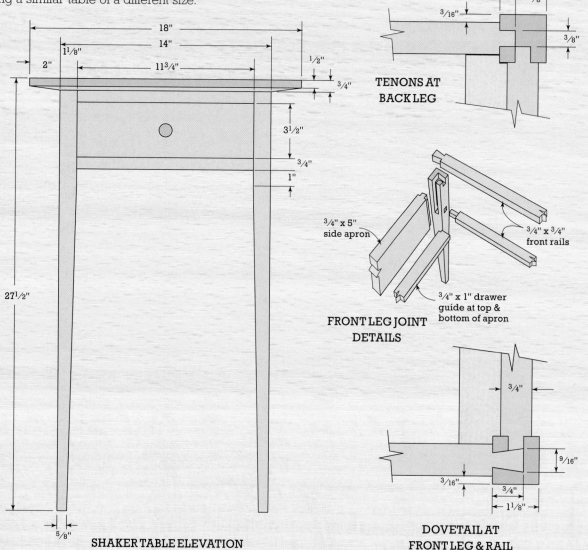

SHAKER TABLE ELEVATION

TENONS AT BACK LEG

³/₄" x 5" side apron

³/₄" x ³/₄" front rails

³/₄" x 1" drawer guide at top & bottom of apron

FRONT LEG JOINT DETAILS

DOVETAIL AT FRONT LEG & RAIL

Arch Table

BY JEFF MILLER

Many interesting pieces of furniture are deceptively simple. Deceptive, because although they appear simple, they are actually very difficult to make. Although this is occasionally true in my own work, that's not the case with the Arch Table, a piece that looks more complicated to make than it actually is. I'm not saying it's easy; there's a lot of preparatory work, and it is quite demanding in terms of shop resources. But the stuff that looks hard to do is actually not all that bad.

This piece is a great introduction to bent lamination, which opens up an entire world of curved shapes and lightweight, incredibly strong components. There are a lot of ways to approach lamination; for this project I make use of table-sawn strips, and rely on forms and cauls for gluing up the curved components. The complex-looking joinery is mostly screwed and glued together. In early versions of this table, I used mortises and tenons for the branching joints, but because of short-grain considerations, I found the screws to be a much stronger solution.

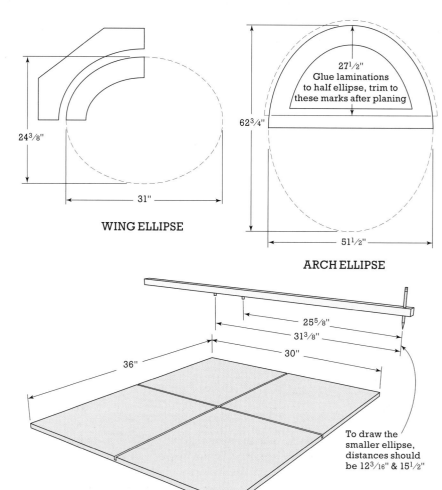

WING ELLIPSE

27½"
Glue laminations to half ellipse, trim to these marks after planing

62¾"

ARCH ELLIPSE

51½"

25⅝"

31⅜"

30"

36"

To draw the smaller ellipse, distances should be 12³⁄₁₆" & 15½"

ELLIPSE-DRAWING JIG

Forms & Cauls

The major prep work is in making the forms for the laminations. For the table's "wings," you'll need to make both a form and a caul (or a pair of each, if you want to speed up the process) for gluing together the layers. For the main arch, it depends on how many clamps you have available. I just glue up around a form with six layers of ¼" Masonite acting as a caul, distributing pressure and preventing dents from the clamps. But I use 26 bar clamps in the process; without that large a collection, you'll definitely need to make up the cauls for a successful glue-up.

Layout for the forms involves drawing sections of some large ellipses. I made up a fairly simple ellipse-drawing jig. You could also draw an ellipse on the computer and print it out full-size then tape the tiled pages together. It's also possible to draw this ellipse with a loop of string and two nails. However you create the shape, it's best to draw directly on a piece of ¾" plywood. Then cut it out as accurately as possible, and smooth to your line. You can also cut out the center section of the form at this time. Accuracy

there is not nearly as important.

Use this first layer of the form to mark out the next two layers (note: you can piece together one of the layers if necessary), and cut them slightly oversized. Then glue and screw these layers to either side of the original, and flush them off using a router and flush-trim bit. Finally, go over the edges with sandpaper to even out any irregularities, then wax the edges plus a little bit of the sides of the form.

To make up cauls, you need to know the overall thickness of your lamination. You should wait until you've actually ripped the strips for that, then clamp together all but one of your strips into a bundle to get an exact thickness (the last strip gets glued on after attaching the wings). With this information, you can make a scribing disk. This disk is used to draw the exact curve needed to apply even clamping pressure to the outside of the bundle of strips all the way around the curve.

The saw is set to rip strips to a precise width at the outside of the cut, which is safer than cutting thin pieces between the blade and the fence.

A paint roller makes quick work of spreading the glue evenly on all of the laminations.

Before you add glue, do a dry run to ensure you've enough clamps – and that when then glue is on, you know where to place them.

I make these disks on the drill press using a fly cutter – one of those rather terrifying circle cutters with an adjustable cross beam and cutter. You want the distance from the edge of the center hole (not the center of this hole) to the outside of the disk to be the same as your lamination thickness.

Set your form down on a piece of $^3/_4$" plywood, and roll the disk around your form with a sharp pencil pressed against the edge of the center hole to mark out the caul. Cut, then smooth carefully to your line, and add two more layers of plywood and flush trim those just as you did for the form itself. If you're doing this for the big arch, you'll ultimately want to break up the caul into three sections to keep it manageable. You'll also want to make registration marks, or even add some wooden registration strips, so the form and cauls will line back up exactly right when the time comes to glue your lamination.

Rip Strips for the Laminations

You will need roughly 16 $^3/_{32}$"-thick strips, ripped from stock that is 1$^7/_8$" to 2" thick, to make up the final thickness of 1$^1/_2$". Mark a layout triangle on the face of your board before you do anything else. I rip the strips on the table saw, and always set up so that I cut the strips to the outside of the blade. This means resetting the fence after each rip (moving it over $^3/_{32}$" plus the thickness of the blade).

Setting the rip fence at $^3/_{32}$" and trying to rip the strips is a major safety problem and can lead to some nasty kickback and shattered strips. Because this constant adjustment of the fence is a pain, it makes sense to cut down your wood into two or three equal widths (try for two pieces at least 3$^3/_4$" wide). That way you can rip more than one board at the same setting. Be aware that it's unsafe to rip strips out of a board that's less than $^1/_2$" wide. Don't even try.

Use a featherboard to press the wood against the fence, but only in front of the blade. You'll also need a push stick handy for when the board gets narrow. Pile up the strips in order as they come off the blade, or in multiple piles if you're cutting from more than one board. If things go awry, you can always put the strips back in order by referring to the layout triangle.

You'll need one less strip for each of the wing bundles than you'll need for the arches; the outer layer will come from the outer layer of the arch, which gets glued on after you join the wings to the arch.

Glue Up the Laminations

Most wood glues have a small amount of flexibility to allow for joint expansion and contraction. When you're gluing together a lamination, however, that flexibility can lead to the layers slipping a bit in relation to their neighbors. This glue-line "creep" can cause the

laminated shape to lose some of its bend (springback), and can create little ridges between layers. The best bet is to use either Weldwood Plastic Resin Glue (a powder and water mix), or Unibond 800 (a powder and liquid mix). Both have rigid gluelines, long open times and work especially well for this type of work. These glues also require caution when working with them; be sure to wear a good dust mask and gloves while mixing, and keep the gloves on throughout the preparation and application.

Before you do anything else, set aside the outermost strip from each of your two main arch bundles. Label these strips so you'll be able to glue them on later in their proper places.

There's a little more preparation needed before you can actually glue up your laminations. First, you'll want to figure out where you can do the glue-up. I work on the floor mostly because I've been doing it that way for 25 years, but my shop floor is completely covered with glue spots; this may not go over so well in your shop. It's also easier to work at a more comfortable height. My knees have been lobbying for this change of late.

Setting up a piece of melamine board (which can be scraped clean when you're done), or plywood on solid sawhorses or benches is probably preferable. Or just cover your floor with cardboard, plastic or paper. You'll also want to protect the floor or set up a second work surface

A form for the outside of the curve helps to spread clamp pressure, reducing the number of clamps needed.

The jointer levels the surface of the lamination. Infeed and outfeed supports help keep the material flat on the machine bed.

where you can roll out the glue on all of the remaining strips.

It pays to go through a dry run to be sure you have everything ready to go and to familiarize yourself with the process. Set your form on top of a few wood blocks sized to make it easier to get the first clamps into place under the form. If you haven't already, prepare the six ¼" × 2" Masonite strips or a set of cauls.

You may want to position a handful of clamps under the form, ready to receive the lamination. In any event, all the clamps should be at hand. Center the bundle of strips on the form, then bend the strips into place for your dry run. Start clamping at the top of the arch and work down the sides, alternating clamps above and below the form as you go.

The actual glue-up starts with laying out all of your strips in order, then separating the top strip from the rest, so you don't accidentally get glue on it. Mix up your glue – about a cup and a half should be enough for the main arch – according to the directions. Then roll the glue onto your strips with a foam paint roller. I don't bother with a paint tray; I just pour

a little glue on the strips and spread it around. Make sure you cover the strips completely, and go over any spots that look a little dry. Stack up the bundle in order (including the top strip), and clamp it to your form as you did during the dry run. Try to keep the edges of the strips reasonably well aligned; it will make smoothing the edges much easier. Let the glue set for at least 12 hours – longer if it's colder than 70° Fahrenheit in your shop. Finally, before you remove the clamps, transfer the marks for the bottoms of the arch from the form onto your laminations.

The process is the same for gluing up the wings.

Smooth the Laminations
When you take the laminations off the forms, they will look like a mess. Before you clean up the edges, move the arch bottom location marks to the inner faces, where you won't cut them away.

Set up infeed and outfeed supports next to your jointer, and joint one of the edges of the lamination. Unfortunately, this is pretty hard on the jointer knives,

The opposite side of the glued lamination is surfaced with the planer.

Arch Table

NO.	ITEM	T	W	L	MATERIAL	COMMENTS
		DIMENSIONS (INCHES)				
2	Large arches	1½	1½	*	Lamination	
4	Wings	1½	1½	*	Lamination	
2	Arched lower rails	¾	2¾	10¾	Solid	1" TBE
2	Angled upper rails	1⅛	4⅜	11¼	Solid	1¼" TBE
3	Top rails	¾	2	11⅝	Solid	1" TBE
2	Angled aprons	1	1⅛	52	Solid	Cut to fit
1	Top	1¼	15	64	Solid	

*Laminated from strips, ³⁄₃₂" × 1⅞" to 2" × 92"; TBE = Tenon, both ends

but I haven't found much else that will do the job as easily and quickly. A few passes and you should have a clean edge. Then you get to pass the lamination through the planer. I know it looks odd, but it does work. Apologies to the planer knives as well.

Joinery

Once the laminations have been machined smooth, it's time to move on to sizing and joinery. The ends of the arches can be cut off at the marks using whatever method works best for you (you can always go back to the forms and re-mark if you forgot that step earlier). An outfeed support will be necessary if you're using the table saw or band saw. Hold off on cutting the wings to length for now.

The joint between the arches and the wings has a routed flat on the arch where the bottom of each wing attaches. The flat begins 16⁹⁄₁₆" up from the bottom of the arch (along the outer curve, or 15¹¹⁄₁₆" measured straight up from the floor) with a ³⁄₃₂" step down to the flat. The flat is roughly 4¹⁄₄" long, and simply feathers out at the top; there is no step there. Start by marking the step-down locations on each side of the two arches. Then at one of those locations, measure down ³⁄₃₂" and draw a line from there to 20¹³⁄₁₆" up on the lamination as a reference for where the flat should end.

Make up a jig for routing the flats as shown in the photo on the next page. Two shims added between the jig and the lamination will set the jig up for the right cut. Put the jig (without shims) in place on top of the lamination, then shim it up so the top of the inner edges is flush with the layout lines for your flat. Glue or tack the shims into place, and you won't have to repeat this process at the other locations. Clamp the jig in place on the lamination.

Set up your router so that a ¹⁄₂" straight (or spiral-upcut) bit just touches the top of the inner surface of the jig. Start the router in an upper corner, safely away from contact with the lamination. Then rout around the edges clockwise (in a gentle climb cut) to give you a clean edge. Go slowly across the step at the bottom so you don't blow out the wood as you exit the cut. Then rout away the remainder of the flat. Finish the other three flats the same way.

Layout for the wings requires a little more work. Do this on a large surface of at least 31" × 55", with a square edge (I used a piece of plywood a little bigger than that). The base of the table actually

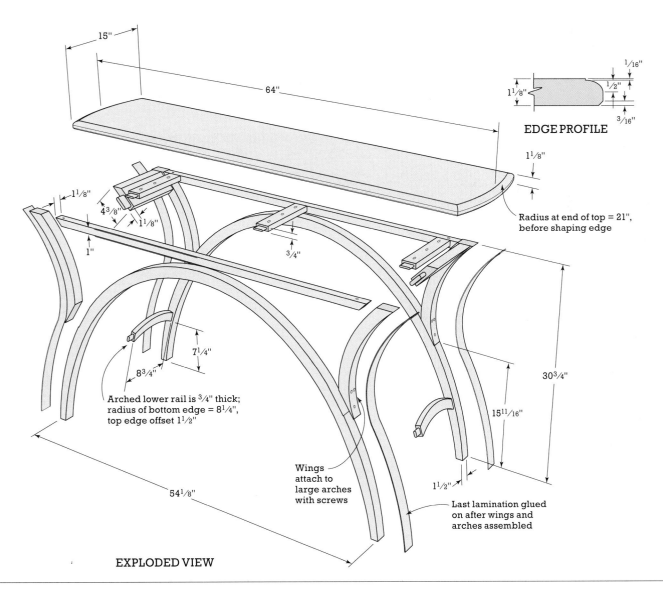

EDGE PROFILE

Radius at end of top = 21", before shaping edge

Arched lower rail is ³⁄₄" thick; radius of bottom edge = 8¹⁄₄", top edge offset 1¹⁄₂"

Wings attach to large arches with screws

Last lamination glued on after wings and arches assembled

EXPLODED VIEW

fits into a rectangle roughly 54" wide by 30¾" tall (your base may vary slightly in from this size).

The ends of the wings are directly above the bottom of the arch (on the outside face). You'll use this to lay out where the flats need to be cut on the wings. Measure 30¾" up from the bottom of the plywood along the square edge and mark a line. Set up the arch on three or four 1½"-thick scraps (I used the lamination offcuts) with the bottom aligned with the bottom edge of the plywood and one side at the square edge. Now take one of the wings and place it on the plywood with the more curved end toward the arch.

The goal is to find a location for the wing that allows the curve to flow well into the bottom of the arch while the top part of the wing touches the edge of the plywood at the 30¾" mark. Once you're satisfied with the location, trace the flat and the step onto the wing. You can also make a mark ½" above the 30¾" line, where you'll be able to trim the top of the wing roughly to size.

Now you need a way to cut the flats on all four of the wings. The easiest way to do this is to create a positioning jig. Start by tracing the inside curve of a wing onto a piece of ¾" plywood, particleboard or MDF, and cut out the shape. Place this curved piece on a larger rectangle of plywood. Move the wing and the curved piece so that the line you marked from the flat of the arch is located over the edge of the rectangular plywood. Confirm the location, then screw the curved piece down. Now, if you set up to cut flush with the edge of the plywood, you can cut each of the wings held in place on this positioning jig just where they need to be cut.

You still have to crosscut the pointy end you just created on each wing so it will match up with the step on the arch. This is an easy crosscut on the table saw using the miter guide with a sacrificial fence. Mark out the cut location, and place the wing's flat down on the saw

table. Clamp to the miter guide so nothing slips, and make the cut.

The main arches need two small mortises each for the stretchers. The basic approach to cutting these joints is to create a simple positioning jig you can clamp into place that will allow you to rout (or use a hollow-chisel mortiser, or drill) as if the part were a rectangle.

Plunge routing requires a wide, stable platform for the router to rest on, so I used a 4"-wide board of the same thickness as my lamination to make the jig. Start by measuring 8⅜" up from the bottom along the outside of the lamination. Mark a line there for the center of the ⅜"-wide × ⅞"-long mortise. The centerline of the mortise will be ¹⁹⁄₃₂" from the outside edge of the arch. This is slightly off center, but there's still another lamination layer to add to the outside of the arch.

The goal now is to mark a cutout in the positioning jig so the outer edge of the jig lines up parallel with where the

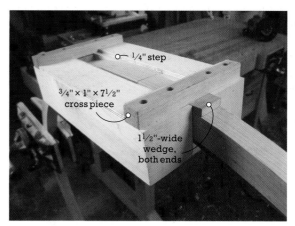

This jig supports a router, used to create a flat surface for the wing to connect with the large arch.

A piece of plywood locates the corners of the large arch and the wings. Mark the wings from the flats on the arches.

Align the straight cut on the wing with the edge of the jig base.

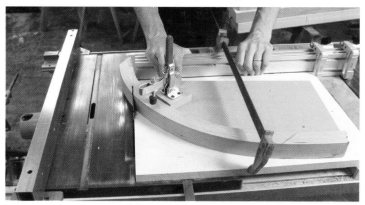

The jig holds the curved part securely to make the cut, creating a flat surface to attach the wing to the arch.

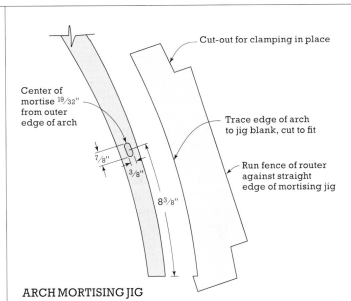

Center of mortise ¹⁹/₃₂" from outer edge of arch

Cut-out for clamping in place

Trace edge of arch to jig blank, cut to fit

Run fence of router against straight edge of mortising jig

⁷/₈"

³/₈"

8³/₈"

ARCH MORTISING JIG

This jig provides a flat reference for the router fence and holds the wing securely to make the mortise.

mortise needs to be (basically tangent to the curve at the centerline of the mortise). Cut out the arch shape, then transfer the mortise location to the jig, and square it around to the other side as well.

Clamp the positioning jig in place, and set up a plunge router with a fence. Set the fence so the ³/₈" × ⁷/₈" mortise will be centered ¹⁹/₃₂" from the outside edge of the arch. You can either transfer marks to the arch and rout by eye, or set up some stops to limit the travel of the router. Rout the mortise roughly 1" deep. I find that a series of very shallow passes gives a more accurate result, with less chatter of the router bit. You can simply flip the jig over to rout the opposite side of the arch.

Drill and countersink three holes in each wing, perpendicular to the flat face. Now screw the wings into place temporarily (no glue!) so you can lay out the tops of the wings and the front and back aprons. The aprons are 1" high, 1¹/₈" wide, and roughly 60" long. Save a couple scraps from milling them so you can prop up the arch for an easier layout. The layout process takes place on the plywood you used to set up the wing alignment. Here, prop up the arch on the scraps at the bottom and the stretcher at the top. Align the bottom of the arch with the bottom of the plywood and clamp it in place.

The apron should be set so the line that is 30³/₄" up from the bottom of the plywood is at its top. Now you can mark the curvature of the wings onto the apron, and the tops of the wings from the top

edge of the apron (use a short pencil stub to mark from underneath). Label each location so you can put everything back together the way you marked it. Carefully saw to your lines. You'll have a chance to rout the tops of the wings flush later, but you should try to smooth the ends of the aprons carefully to fit the wings. You can undercut the center portion of the apron's ends a little bit if you like.

Mortising the upper part of the wings for the side aprons is very similar to mortising the arch for the lower stretchers. Make a similar positioning jig with a straight edge parallel to the mortise you need, then locate the mortise by referencing off that edge. These mortises should be ¹/₂" × 2" × 1¹/₄" deep.

Shaping & Smoothing
Lay out a curved taper on the inside of the arches, starting opposite the wing

joint and tapering down to 1" wide at the bottom of the arch. You can use the outside of the other arch to draw this curved taper. Band saw the waste off, then smooth the curve. This can be a little tricky, because the glue lines are harder to cut than the wood, but a sharp spokeshave followed by a scraper usually does the trick. Sandpaper on an appropriately curved sanding block will work, too. While you're at it, smooth out the rest of the arch and the convex parts of the wings and chamfer the very bottoms of the arches' "feet."

Assembly
It's finally time to attach the wings to the arch. Glue and screw them into position and plug the holes. Then refine the transition (and flush off the plugs) with a spokeshave, rasp, scraper and/or sanding block so you'll be able to glue and clamp the

The final strip covers the joint, leaving uninterrupted grain on the outside of the assembly.

Clean up the transition between the wing and the arch to provide a smooth bed for the last laminate.

This jig provides a flat surface for the router base, bringing the front-to-back rails and the tops of the wings flush with the aprons.

A router bit won't reach the inside corner to shape the edge. Carve into the corner from both directions.

final layer to the outside of the arch and wing. Be careful not to round over this surface from side to side or you'll never be able to glue the final layer on effectively. Check to be sure that the outside strip will actually conform to the refined curve and adjust as necessary. Then cut the outer strips so that they are a few inches longer than needed. They should remain wider than the laminations to leave some room for misalignment.

It takes a lot of smaller clamps to glue on the final layers. I only do one of the four glue-ups at a time. I use ¼" Masonite strips or extra sliced layers as cauls and to protect the inside of the arch from the clamps. I also screw some shaped blocks to the Masonite to help position some of the clamps appropriately. A dry run will help you figure out what you need to do to stay in control when the glue is finally applied.

When the glue is dry, cut the excess length, plane off the excess width and finish smoothing out all of the edges as well. There are probably little bits of the routed flat sections above where the wings attach to the arches. A bit of sandpaper backed up by a thin scraper makes it easy to get in there to ease that transition. Round over all of the edges with a ¼" roundover bit set to about two-thirds of its normal depth, then follow this up by carving, filing and sanding the inside corners of the arch-to-wing intersections.

Mill the side apron and lower

stretcher blanks. Cut and fit the tenons. Then band saw and smooth the lower stretchers to shape. Make sure to ease the bottom corners of the stretchers a little to avoid the short-grain weakness there. Then round over the edges to match the arches. Bevel the tops of the aprons to roughly the angle of the wings, but leave them a little long for now.

Drill countersunk pilot holes – essentially pocket holes – in the ends of the front and back aprons so you can attach them to the wings. These should be roughly perpendicular to the angled ends of the stretchers. You also need to mortise the inside faces of these aprons for three crosspieces you'll use to attach the tabletop to the base. You can determine the length of these crosspieces by dry-fitting the arch assemblies and the aprons together, then setting the front and back aprons in place centered on the width of the wings. Measure the distance between aprons, then add the tenon lengths to get the overall lengths.

Cut and tenon the crosspieces, then drill them for the screws to attach the top. The center holes can be left as-is, but the holes to the front and back should be elongated to allow for expansion and contraction of the solid top. Smooth any

components that still need attention.

Glue up the arches with the lower stretchers and side aprons. Separately, glue up the front and back aprons and the crosspieces. Once the arch is out of clamps, you can screw the upper apron assembly in place. I flush off the tops of the aprons and legs using a large piece of plywood that has a rectangular opening that fits over the ends of the legs and end apron. I clamp this in place on the front and back aprons, then rout away anything that projects above the height of those aprons. Be sure to use a light climb cut to avoid blowing out the edges.

Making the top is nothing out of the ordinary. Shape the end curves on the band saw set up with adequate support to the side. Plane everything smooth, then rout and smooth the edge profile on top and bevel the underside. You can screw the top on now, but I usually wait until after finishing the table; it's much easier to finish the top and base separately. I finish with five or more coats of an oil/varnish blend followed by a coat of wax, but any finish you're comfortable with will work.

After shaping and finishing the top, attach it to the base with screws through the front-to-back rails.

Distributed in Canada by Fraser Direct
100 Armstrong Avenue
Georgetown, Ontario L7G 5S4
Canada

Distributed in the U.K. and Europe by
F&W Media International, LTD
Brunel House, Ford Close
Newton Abbot
TQ12 4PU, UK
Tel: (+44) 1626 323200
Fax: (+44) 1626 323319

Distributed in Australia by Capricorn Link
P.O. Box 704
Windsor, NSW 2756
Australia

Visit our website at popularwoodworking.com or our consumer website at shopwoodworking.com for more woodworking information projects.

Other fine Popular Woodworking Books are available from your local bookstore or direct from the publisher.

ISBN-13: 978-1-4403-4052-9

18 17 16 15 14   5 4 3 2 1

Editor: Robert W. Lang
Designer: Daniel T. Pessell
Production coordinator: Debbie Thomas

About the Authors

MEGAN FITZPATRICK
Megan is the editor of *Popular Woodworking Magazine*, and has written and edited numerous articles on the craft in her decade of woodworking.

GLEN D. HUEY
Glen is a former managing editor of *Popular Woodworking Magazine*. He is the author of a number of books on building furniture, and teaches and hosts DVDs about furniture building.

BILL HYLTON
Bill is a longtime woodworker and writer, best known for his authoritative books on cabinetmaking and router use.

ROBERT W. LANG
Bob is a former executive editor with *Popular Woodworking Magazine* and has been a professional woodworker since the early 1970s. He is the author of several *Shop Drawings* books.

JEFF MILLER
Jeff is a furniture designer, craftsman, and teacher, as well as the author of several books and many articles on woodworking.

DARRELL PEART
Darrell got his start in woodworking making small items for sale in Seattle's Pike Place Market. Since then, he's become recognized as an authority on Greene & Greene furniture, and has written several books on the subject.

KERRY PIERCE
Kerry has been a frequent contributor to *Popular Woodworking Magazine* and is the author of a number of books on Shaker furniture.

MARIO RODRIGUEZ
Mario has more than 30 years' experience as woodworker, teacher and writer. He now is co-owner of the Philadelphia Furniture Workshop.

CHRISTOPHER SCHWARZ
Chris is a former editor of *Popular Woodworking Magazine* (now contributing editor) and is the editor at Lost Art Press.

MATTHEW TEAGUE
Matthew worked for *Fine Woodworking* and *Popular Woodworking Magazine*, and is now editorial director at Spring House Press.

TROY SEXTON
Troy is a professional woodworker and a former contributing editor for *Popular Woodworking Magazine*.

JOHN TATE
John was an intern at *Popular Woodworking Magazine*, and jumped head first into the craft during his time on staff.

Metric Conversion Chart

TO CONVERT	TO	MULTIPLY BY
Inches	Centimeters	2.54
Centimeters	Inches	0.4
Feet	Centimeters	30.5
Centimeters	Feet	0.03
Yards	Meters	0.9
Meters	Yards	1.1

Read This Important Safety Notice

To prevent accidents, keep safety in mind while you work. Use the safety guards installed on power equipment; they are for your protection.

When working on power equipment, keep fingers away from saw blades, wear safety goggles to prevent injuries from flying wood chips and sawdust, wear hearing protection and consider installing a dust vacuum to reduce the amount of airborne sawdust in your woodshop.

Don't wear loose clothing, such as neckties or shirts with loose sleeves, or jewelry, such as rings, necklaces or bracelets, when working on power equipment. Tie back long hair to prevent it from getting caught in your equipment.

People who are sensitive to certain chemicals should check the chemical content of any product before using it.

Due to the variability of local conditions, construction materials, skill levels, etc., neither the author nor Popular Woodworking Books assumes any responsibility for any accidents, injuries, damages or other losses incurred resulting from the material presented in this book.

The authors and editors who compiled this book have tried to make the contents as accurate and correct as possible. Plans, illustrations, photographs and text have been carefully checked. All instructions, plans and projects should be carefully read, studied and understood before beginning construction.

Prices listed for supplies and equipment were current at the time of publication and are subject to change.

IDEAS • INSTRUCTION • INSPIRATION

These are other great Popular Woodworking products are available at your local bookstore, woodworking store or online supplier.

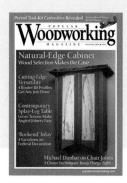

Popular Woodworking Magazine

Get must-build projects, information on tools (both hand and power) and their use and technique instruction in every issue of *Popular Woodworking Magazine*. Each issue (7 per year) includes articles and expert information from some of the best-known names in woodworking. Subscribe today at popularwoodworking.com.

Subscription • 7 issues/year

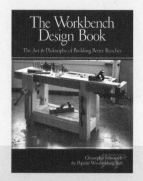

The Workbench Design Book
By Christopher Schwarz

How many times have you heard this: "The workbench is the most important tool in your shop." While the statement is absolutely true, it doesn't help you answer the more important question: Which workbench should you build? This book explores that problem with a depth and detail you won't find in any other source in print or online.

Hardcover • 256 pages

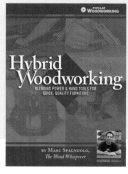

Hybrid Woodworking
By Marc Spagnuolo

Known online as The Wood Whisperer, Marc Spaguolo presents a fresh approach to woodworking and furniture making by showing the most efficient ways to utilize both power tools and hand tools in the furniture building process. Not only will you learn which tools are best for which tasks, but you will also find tips for how to use, maintain, and fine tune them.

Paperback • 192 pages

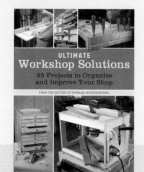

Ultimate Workshop Solutions
By Popular Woodworking Editors

From better clamp storage, to benches and beyond, you'll find 35 projects specifically designed to improve and organize your favorite space. These projects have been created by the editors of *Popular Woodworking Magazine* for your shop, and now we're pleased to share them with you.

Paperback • 192 pages

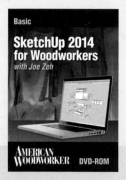

Basic Sketch-Up For Woodworkers
By Joe Zeh

SketchUp has helped thousands of woodworkers create, correct and perfect their furniture designs before the first piece of expensive wood is cut. Now Joe Zeh, an expert in Sketchup and Computer-Aided Design (CAD) will show you the brand-new 2014 edition and how much easier and more versatile it is to use.

**Available at Shopwoodworking.com
DVD**

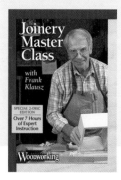

Joinery Master Class With Frank Klausz
By Frank Klausz

Frank Klausz, expert craftsmen and experienced woodworking teacher, shares with you on this 2-DVD set the joinery skills he's learned in a lifetime (edge-joint options, bridle joints, dovetails, mortise-and-tenon variations and more!). Plus five projects to help you put your joinery knowledge into practice.

**Available at Shopwoodworking.com
DVD & download**

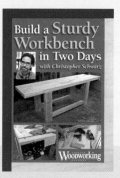

Build A Sturdy Workbench In Two Days
By Christopher Schwarz

With a base built from standard 4x4 lumber, a base with half-lap construction, and a top made from two IKEA countertops, this two-day workbench is a seriously sturdy shop workhorse that no one will question for quality. With this solid workbench, you'll have no shortage of working surface or dog holes.

**Available at Shopwoodworking.com
DVD & download**

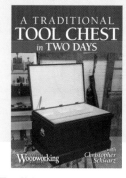

A Traditional Tool Chest In Two Days
By Christopher Schwarz

Woodworkers who use traditional tool chests swear they're the most convenient way to organize tools. Now, you can make one in just two days using modern materials and contemporary joinery techniques. Whether your focus is hand tool or power tool woodworking, you'll find this tool chest indispensable (a quick to build!).

**Available at Shopwoodworking.com
DVD & download**

Visit **popularwoodworking.com** to see more woodworking information by the experts, learn about our digital subscription and sign up to receive our free newsletter or blog posts.